GREAT MEDIEVAL CHURCHMEN
Edited by
L. ELLIOTT BINNS, D.D.

NICHOLAS OF CUSA

BAS RELIEF, BY ANDREA BREGNO, ON MONUMENT OF NICHOLAS OF CUSA
IN HIS TITULAR CHURCH OF S. PIETRO IN VINCOLI AT ROME

SHOWING S. PETER HOLDING HIS FETTERS, WITH THE ANGEL OF DELIVERANCE KNEELING AT
HIS LEFT HAND, AND NICHOLAS AT HIS RIGHT HAND

NICHOLAS OF CUSA

BY

HENRY BETT, M.A.

HANDSWORTH COLLEGE, BIRMINGHAM

WITH A PORTRAIT

METHUEN & CO. LTD.
36 ESSEX STREET W.C.
LONDON

First Published in 1932

PRINTED IN GREAT BRITAIN

GENERAL PREFACE

THE aim of the series as a whole is to produce a number of studies of various leading medieval Churchmen, more particularly of those who have not yet received their rightful meed of appreciation. These studies will attempt to view their subjects, not in isolation, but as contributing to the Church's life and thought at some particular epoch.

The responsibility of the general editor has been confined to the choice of subjects and authors : in his own volume each of the latter has been allowed full liberty both of judgement and method.

L. E. B.

AUTHOR'S PREFACE

IT is rather strange that no English book has existed hitherto on so important a thinker as Nicholas of Cusa. This volume may therefore claim to be at least a serious attempt to fill a real gap.

I should like to acknowledge the constant courtesy of the officials of the Reading Room at the British Museum, and of the University Library at Manchester, on my numberless visits to these institutions for years past.

Last, I would make a grateful acknowledgement of the kindness of my friend and former colleague, the Rev. W. F. Flemington, M.A., who has read the proofs of the volume.

H. B.

CONTENTS

PART I
THE LIFE OF NICHOLAS OF CUSA

PART II
THE WRITINGS OF NICHOLAS OF CUSA

PART III
THE PHILOSOPHY OF NICHOLAS OF CUSA

NICHOLAS OF CUSA

I

THE LIFE OF NICHOLAS OF CUSA

CHAPTER I

EARLY LIFE AND THE COUNCIL OF BASEL

NICHOLAS OF CUSA was one of the most remarkable men of the fifteenth century. His ecclesiastical career is one of great interest and great importance, for he lived through a period of crisis in the history of the Church, which was largely prophetic of the greater events of the next century, and his own part in the affairs of his age was very considerable. But his principal importance belongs to the world of thought rather than to the world of action. As a philosopher, he wrought out an intellectual system which is as profound as it is subtle, and which possesses a peculiar importance because of its unique relation, on the one hand, to the philosophy of the Middle Ages, and on the other, to the philosophy of the Renaissance and of modern times.

The beginning of the fifteenth century was a remarkable juncture in the history of Europe.

There were still two rival Popes, Boniface IX at
Rome, and Benedict XIII at Avignon, who divided
between them the spiritual allegiance of the West,
though various attempts had been made for years
past to restore the unity of the Church.   The state
of the Empire was scarcely more creditable than
that of the Church, for Wenceslaus of Bohemia, a
drunken madman, had reigned for more than
twenty years past, until he was deposed in August
1400, when Rupert of the Palatinate was elected
in his place.   It would scarcely be fanciful to regard
these things as omens, for the medieval system
represented by the Church and the Empire was
beginning to break down.   Both the Pope and
the Emperor were to recover some prestige during the next generation or two, but as we look
back we can see many indications that the old
régime was doomed, and that it was about to be
submerged by the rising tide of nationalism.

There was a singular inconsistency in the intellectual aspect of the time.   It saw the very end
of the scholasticism and mysticism of the Middle
Ages, and it saw the very beginning of the new
learning of the Renaissance and the new liberty
of the Reformation.   When Nicholas of Cusa was
born Tauler had been dead for forty years, and
Ruysbroeck for twenty, while Thomas à Kempis
was his contemporary.   Wyclif had passed away
in peace at Lutterworth nearly twenty years before,
and Hus was to be martyred at Constance fifteen
years later.   The new learning was being introduced in Nicholas's lifetime by men like Bessarion,
Gemistus Pletho, George of Trebizond, and Laurentius Valla.   Gabriel Biel, almost the last repre-

sentative of scholasticism, outlived Nicholas, and Erasmus was born within a year or two of the Cardinal's death.

Nicholas was born in 1401, at the village of Cues, on the left bank of the Moselle, opposite Berncastel, about forty-five miles above Coblenz, and about twenty-five miles below Trèves. The father of Nicholas was Johann Cryfts,[1] who survived until 1450 or 1451 ; his mother, Catherina Roemer, who came from Bredel near Zell,[2] died in 1427. Johann Cryfts was a well-to-do boatowner (*nauta*), who at his death possessed houses, vineyards, fields, and other property, worth 3,000 Rhenish gold florins, the equivalent of about £3,000 to-day.[3] When the Cardinal made his will, and founded the hospital of St. Nicholas for poor men in Cues (which still exists), there was an agreement by which his brother John and his sister Clara consented to forgo their share of his property [4] ; the hospital still owns

[1] Cryfts, Cryftz, Chrypffs, Krypffs, or Kribshenne (i.e. Hans Krebs). The name is still common in the vicinity of Cues. The equivalent in modern German is Krebs, and a crab *gules* on a field *argent* was borne on the Cardinal's coat of arms.

[2] Scharpff, *Der Cardinal und Bischof Nicolaus von Cusa*, p. 11. Scharpff wrote two books on Nicholas—the one just mentioned, which I shall henceforth cite as : Scharpff, *Nicolaus von Cusa*, and another entitled *Der Cardinal und Bischof Nicolaus von Cues als Reformator in Kirche, Reich und Philosophie*, which I shall cite as : Scharpff, *Reformator*.

[3] Marx, *Nikolaus von Cues und seine Stiftungen zu Cues und Deventer*, p. 134.

[4] His younger brother John was a priest at Berncastel, and died on the 7th of May 1456. His sister Margaret married a magistrate of Trèves, whose name was Matthias, and died young. His sister Clara married, first, a citizen of Trèves,

some vineyards in the neighbourhood of Cues. These details prove that the family of Nicholas was reasonably prosperous.

We know nothing of Nicholas's boyhood except the story that the boy fled from his father's harshness and sought refuge with Count Theodoric von Manderscheid.[1] It is said that his father, provoked by the boy's studious habits, and his ineptitude for the business of the river, knocked him overboard with a blow of the oar. The place where this is said to have happened is still called by the country-folk the Schmeissgraben [2] —a strong confirmation of the story, for the popular memory is surprisingly retentive in details of this sort.

The tradition is that the Count von Manderscheid sent the boy to the famous school of the Brothers of the Common Life at Deventer—the school where both Thomas à Kempis and Erasmus were

John Plynisch, and, second, a magistrate of the same city, Paul von Brystge, who was burgomaster from 1458 until his death ten years later. The Cardinal describes her in an autobiographical manuscript, as *Uxor Pauli de Brysig scabini et sculteti Trevirensis* (Uebinger, *Zur Lebensgeschichte des Nikolaus Cusanus*, in the *Görres-Gesellschaft Historisches Jahrbuch*, xiv (1893), p. 550). She died on the 8th of September 1473. Her tombstone is on the northern side of the Chapel of the Hospital at Cues.

[1] His gratitude to the family manifested itself later in his ardent advocacy of the claims of Ulric von Manderscheid to the archbishopric of Trèves at the Council of Basel. In founding the hospital at Cues, too, he left a room in the nobles' quarter at the disposition of Count Theodoric von Manderscheid-Schleiden and his heirs. Marx, *Stiftungen*, p. 140.

[2] Marx, *Stiftungen*, p. 136.

educated. The fact is not quite certain, but there are several circumstances which make it seem highly probable. Nothing is known of his life at school, but if it is a fact that he was educated under such auspices it is a very significant one. The mystical strain which is so strong in him, his dependence upon Eckhart, and indeed the whole cast of his philosophy would seem to date back to the school at Deventer.

Early in 1416 Nicholas matriculated at the University of Heidelberg,[1] along with nine other clerks of the diocese of Trèves. Rather more than a year later, in October 1417, he migrated to Padua. Little is known of his life at either University. The intellectual atmosphere at Heidelberg was strongly Nominalist, in matters of philosophy, and strongly conciliar, in matters of ecclesiastical politics. Possibly Nicholas was influenced in both directions. At Padua it is certain that he was specially affected by several members of the professoriate,[2] especially Prosdocimo de' Beldomandi,[3] the mathematician and astrologer, Ugo Benzi, the brilliant Hellenist, and most of all by Julian Cesarini, the canonist, a man of noble character,[4] in later years his friend and patron. At this period, Padua was the most famous of the Universities of

[1] The record of his matriculation is extant, and reads *Nicolaus Cancer de Coesze cler(icus) dioc(esis)*. Marx, *Stiftungen*, p. 141. The University had been founded thirty years before, in 1386.

[2] Vansteenberghe, *Nicolas de Cues*, pp. 10–11.

[3] Cantor, *Vorlesungen über die Geschichte der Mathematik*, ii, pp. 186–8.

[4] Pastor, *Geschichte der Päpste*, i, pp. 203–4; Scharpff, *Nicolaus von Cusa*, p. 18; Gibbon, *Decline and Fall*, vii, p. 147.

Italy,[1] only rivalled by Bologna.   It was under Venetian rule at the time when Nicholas was a student.
Besides Cesarini, he made there another life-long
friend, Paolo Toscanelli, the physician of Florence
—*Paulus magistri Domenici, physicus Florentinus*—
who possessed a great store of scientific and
especially of mathematical knowledge.[2]   Toscanelli
was with the Cardinal when he died, forty years later.

Averroism ruled the school of philosophy at

[1] Padova, il cui studio era allora de' più famosi e de più
frequentati di' tutta Europa.   Rossi, *Niccolò di Cusa e la
Direzione Monistica della Filosofia nel Rinascimento*, p. 9.   See
also Rotta, *Il Cardinale Nicolò di Cusa*, p. 10.

[2] Marx, *Stiftungen*, p. 169.   Paolo dal Pozzo Toscanelli
was born at Florence in 1397, and died there in 1482.   He
entered the University of Padua at the age of eighteen,
about the time when Nicholas went there.   He appears also
to have left at about the same time as the future Cardinal,
having graduated in medicine.   He returned to Florence and
spent the rest of his days there, except for short journeys in
the neighbourhood, and visits to Todi and Rome, many of
these last, we may be sure, for the express purpose of visiting the Cardinal.   Nicholas refers to their long and intimate
friendship, in the dedication of one of his mathematical
treatises written in 1450: Quanto me ab annis juventutis
atque adolescentiae nostrae strictori amicitiae nodo atque
cordiali quodam amplexu indesinenter contrinxisti, tanto
nunc, etc.   *De transmutationibus geometricis*, p. 939.

Scharpff (*Reformator*, p. 102) writes of ' a certain Paulus ',
who is evidently something of a mystery to him.   He also
alters *magistri Dominici* to *magisterii Dominici*, because the
original phrase does not seem to him to yield any sense.
It does, of course ; it is an ellipsis describing Toscanelli's
parentage.   ' Er bezeichnet nämlich die Herkunft des als
Arzt und Astronom gleich beruhmten Toscanelli, es ist zu
dem Genetiv in Gedanken ein *filius* hinzusetzen.'   Uebinger,
Zur Lebengeschichte des Nikolaus Cusanus, p. 558, in *Historisches Jahrbuch der Görres-Gesellschaft*, Bd. 14, 1893.

Padua,[1] where Paolo Niccoletti d'Udine [2] was the professor, *in philosophia aristotelica nulli suo tempore in Italia secundus*, as Trithemius declared. Later in life Nicholas criticized the doctrine both of Averroes and of Aristotle. In 1423, after six years of study, Nicholas graduated as Doctor in Canon Law (*decretorum doctor*) at the early age of twenty-three. Almost immediately he journeyed to Rome, about the end of the Jubilee year.[3] He mentions in one of his sermons that he had seen Martin V there, and that he had heard St. Bernardino of Siena preaching in the streets.

On his return to his own country, he entered the University of Cologne, which had been founded about forty years earlier. He was admitted on the 8th of April 1425.[4] Although not yet a priest, he had been collated by the Archbishop of Trèves to the cure of Altrich on the 31st of January 1425, and the generous prelate had also given him a pension of forty florins, and an allowance of wheat and wine.[5] Before the end of the year the Arch-

[1] Padova, sede in quel tempo della tradizione averroistica italiana. Rotta, *Il Pensiero di Nicolò da Cusa*, p. 97.

[2] Vansteenberghe, *Nicolas de Cues*, p. 12.

[3] Nicholas makes a casual reference to people flocking to Rome for the Jubilee, in one of the early paragraphs of the *De mente*, i, p. 147.

[4] Again the record is extant. *Nic(olaus) de Cusa, Dr. iur(is) can(onici) Trev(erensis) d(iocesis)* ; *n(ihil) dedit ob rev(erentiam) pers(one), sed i(uravit) c(omplete)*. The special treatment was owing to his doctorate : ' weil Krebs Doktor des kanonischen Rechtes ist, werden ihm die Immatrikulationsgelder sogar erlassen '. Marx, *Stiftungen*, p. 145.

[5] According to a manuscript in the hand of Nicholas : 40 *florenos, unum plaustrum vini*, 4 *maldra siliginis*. Nicholas quaintly records that on the day after the appointment to

bishop had also given Nicholas a canonry at the
Church of St. Simeon in Trèves. But already he
was marked out for the work of ecclesiastical
diplomacy. Cardinal Giordano Orsini, who was
legate in Germany, saw a legal paper prepared by
Nicholas, among the documents of a case con-
cerning the chapter of St. Andrew in Cologne, and
gave judgement accordingly. He entered into
relations with the young canonist, and made him
his secretary.[1] Thus Nicholas was launched upon
his career of ecclesiastical politics.

While Nicholas was acting as secretary to Cardinal Orsini, and while he was attending the
Council of Basel, he was in contact with a number
of Italian humanists. There are several references,
in the correspondence of Poggio and other scholars,
to Nicholas's supposed discoveries of important
classical manuscripts. All of importance that
Nicholas really did achieve in this direction, it
would appear, was the discovery of a manuscript
of Plautus, containing twenty comedies, twelve of
which had been unknown in the Middle Ages.[2]
But while Nicholas was touched with the classical

Altkirch (along with this grant) was made, he saw a camel
at Cues! Marx, *Stiftungen*, p. 145.

[1] This has been doubted in the past, but the researches
of some German and Italian scholars have established the
fact beyond question. See Vansteenberghe, *Nicolas de Cues*,
p. 17, and the authorities quoted there.

[2] Viz. *Bacchides, Mostellaria, Menaechmi, Miles Gloriosus,
Mercator, Pseudolos, Poenulus, Persa, Rudens, Stichus, Trinum-
mus, Truculentus.* The manuscript, which is of the eleventh
century, is known as the Orsinian codex, and is in the Vatican
Library. Rotta, *Il Cardinale Nicolò di Cusa*, p. 18; Vansteenberghe, *Nicolas de Cues*, p. 20.

enthusiasm of the time, he was not a humanist in the sense that some of his acquaintances and friends were. He was an ecclesiastical statesman, first and last, as far as his public career was concerned. That career cannot possibly be understood apart from the state of the Church at the time. And that, again, cannot be understood without some reference to at least three things which were considerable factors in the general situation—the long absence of the Popes from Rome, the existence of the anti-Popes, and the Hussite movement in Bohemia.

Clement V took up his residence at Avignon in the year 1309, and for the next seventy years that city was the seat of the Popes. The mere fact of the long sojourn of the Popes at Avignon —*l'empia Babilonia*, as Petrarch called it—was a great scandal to Christendom. It was universally known that the Popes were almost in vassalage to the French monarchy; the nearness of Avignon to the kingdom of France and the sustained majority of French Cardinals secured that. The result was that the Papacy lost moral prestige, because it had lost spiritual independence. Moreover, the fact that the Popes were absent from their Roman territories reduced one considerable source of income, and made them more than ever avaricious of annates and other Papal tributes, and more than ever unscrupulous as to exacting them. Thus began a widespread distrust and discontent throughout Europe.

This was deeply accentuated by the greater scandal of the Papal schism. Urban VI, who was elected in April 1378, exasperated most of the

Cardinals to the pitch of rebellion by his severity. They retired to Anagni, declared his election invalid, on the ground of compulsion by the Roman populace, and in September at Fondi proceeded to elect Robert of Geneva, who took the style of Clement VII. He soon retired to Avignon, and put himself under French protection. He was recognized by France, Scotland, Savoy, Naples, Lorraine, Navarre, Castile, and Aragon. England, Germany, Hungary, Poland, Denmark and Sweden remained loyal to Urban. Urban was succeeded by Boniface IX, and Clement by Benedict XIII. On the death of Boniface, in 1404, the Italian Cardinals elected Innocent VII, and on his death, in 1408, they elected Gregory XII. Various fruitless efforts to end the schism were made by Charles VI of France, and Wenceslaus of Bohemia. At length under pressure from France on the one side, and the Cardinals at Rome on the other, both Popes agreed upon an interview at Savona in September 1407. Benedict appeared there, but Gregory only went as far as Lucca, and then began negotiations as to another place of meeting. This broken pledge disgusted Gregory's Cardinals, who renounced their allegiance to him. At the same time France renounced allegiance to Benedict, who fled to Perpignan. The Cardinals of both obediences united at Leghorn, and summoned a General Council to meet at Pisa in 1409 for the purpose of re-uniting the Church.

The Council of Pisa opened on the 25th of March 1409. The main purpose of it was to end the schism, but the more enlightened members of the Council wished to seize the occasion to effect general reforms in the Church. The Council deposed both Popes, Gregory and Benedict, and elected the Cardinal Archbishop of Milan, who took the name of Alexander V. Six weeks later the Council was dissolved, having postponed the consideration of reform to a new Council which was to meet in 1412. The result of the Council of Pisa was confusion worse confounded. Neither Gregory nor Benedict acknowledged the legality of the deposition, and so instead of two Popes there were three. During the next few years things went from bad to worse, until Ladislas of Naples occupied Rome and drove John XXIII, who had succeeded Alexander V, to find refuge in Florence. Then the Pope sought the assistance of the Emperor Sigismund, who had personal reasons for opposing Ladislas. Sigismund would only help on condition that the Pope summoned a new Council which should meet in some German city, and end the schism. The Pope reluctantly agreed, and a Council was summoned at Constance, which met in November 1414.

The Council extorted from the Pope a pledge of immediate abdication. He violated his oath, and fled disguised to Schaffhausen. The Council cited him to appear, and then, ten days later, on the 12th of May 1415, solemnly deposed him. Two months later Benedict XIII was deposed and degraded, and Gregory XII withdrew his claims. On the 11th of November 1417, the Cardinals, assisted by the prelates, elected a new Pope, the Cardinal Otto Colonna, the only pontiff of the great Ghibelline house of Rome, who took the style of Martin V. He promised to help forward a general reformation of the Church, but six months after his election he used his authority to dissolve the Council. One of its decrees, however, had provided for the sequence of future councils, and much as Martin V disliked the arrangement, he dared not disregard it utterly. A Council met, therefore, in 1423, first at Pavia, and then, in consequence of the plague, at Siena. The Council did little beyond providing that its successor should meet at Basel in 1431.

The next factor in the situation was the Hussite movement in Bohemia. Strangely enough, this was the direct result of Papal diplomacy. Charles V desired to marry his son to Anne, the sister of Wenceslaus of Bohemia. But the kingdom of France was in ecclesiastical allegiance with Clement VII at Avignon—the anti-Pope elected by French influence—while England and Bohemia were loyal to Urban VI at Rome. The Roman Pope, therefore, used his influence to thwart this projected union, and to bring about the marriage of Anne with Richard II of England, which took place on the 14th of January 1382. The result was a good deal of intercourse between the English and Bohemian Courts, and the Bohemians who passed to and fro between Prague and London carried home with them copies of Wyclif's theological works. These were eagerly read and discussed in the University of Prague, and when translated into Bohemian, among the people of Bohemia in general, and the Hussite movement was the result.

After the martyrdom of Hus at the Council of Constance, in July 1415, events in Bohemia moved rapidly. The whole nation was stirred. Jakubek of Mies, who was priest of the Church of St. Michael at Prague, began to administer the cup in the Mass to the laity, a reform which Hus, in his examination before the Council, had declared to be desirable. From this time forth the necessity of receiving the communion under both kinds was one of the leading tenets of the Bohemian reformers, and the chalice became the symbol of the movement. The followers of Hus, persecuted by the Catholic clergy, gathered together for defence under the leadership of two nobles, John Ziska, and Nicholas of Hussinecz. Upon the death of Wenceslaus, in 1419, there was a general outbreak. The Estates of Bohemia began negotiations with the Emperor Sigismund, but were repulsed. The Pope proclaimed a Crusade against the Bohemians on the 1st of March 1420. Ziska defeated, one after another, bodies of troops sent against him by the Queen, and at Witkow, near Prague, repulsed an attack by the imperial army under Sigismund, who made no further attempt at the time, but passed on to Prague, where he was crowned King of Bohemia on the 28th of July 1420. Later the Taborites, as Ziska's followers were called, occupied Prague, and instituted a rule of puritanical rigour. When this caused discontent, and an insurrection, Ziska withdrew from the city. Sigismund, encouraged by this, ventured to approach Prague once more, but the Taborites, under Hussinecz, inflicted a shameful defeat upon him, and he fled into Hungary. In the meantime doctrinal disputes made their appearance amongst the Bohemians, some of them merely maintaining the Utraquist position, some of them holding much more radical opinions with respect to the Eucharist, and others developing a variety of degenerate superstitions.

There were various futile attempts at a settlement, much fighting, and constant changes in the situation. Finally Cardinal Cesarini, the friend and patron of Nicholas of Cusa, preached a new crusade against the Bohemians, and Sigismund urged it upon the princes and estates of the empire at a Diet held at Nuremburg in 1428. A vast army was assembled, one hundred and thirty thousand strong, under the command of Frederick of Brandenburg. It invaded Bohemia, laying waste the country in its progress, and committing the most fearful excesses. The Hussites came up with the Imperialists near Tauss, on the 14th of August 1431, and, notwithstanding their enormous inferiority in numbers, gained an overwhelming victory. Cesarini, who bore himself bravely throughout, escaped with difficulty in disguise.

Meanwhile the Pope had summoned a Council to meet at Basel in 1431 (in accordance with the decision of the Council of Siena, eight years before) and had appointed Cardinal Cesarini to preside as his representative. A fortnight before the opening of the Council the Pope died, and was succeeded by Gabriel Condulmier, who took the style of Eugenius IV. The new Pope confirmed the appointment of Cesarini. The Council should have opened on the 4th of March, but on that date only one delegate had appeared. Several more appeared during the next few weeks, including three representatives from the University of Paris. The Council actually opened on the 23rd of July, in the Cathedral, with about a dozen representatives present. Cesarini did not appear until six weeks later. He took his seat as president of the assembly on the 9th of September, a month after his escape from the rout at Tauss. Meanwhile the Council had been presided over by his deputies, John of Palomar and John of Ragusa.[1] Cesarini presided over the first public session on the 14th of December.[2]

The Council of Basel marked the beginning of the public career of Nicholas of Cusa. He went there with a very definite commission. He was in charge of the appeal of Ulric von Manderscheid to the Council. On the death of Otho, the Archbishop of Trèves, in 1430, the chapter of Trèves had elected one of its own members, Jakob von Sierck, to the vacant see. Ulric, who was Dean of Cologne, was also a candidate, and being strongly supported by the local nobility, refused to accept the decision of the chapter. Sierck went to Rome to defend the validity of his election, but Martin V conferred the see on Raban, the Bishop of Spires. Ulric now succeeded in securing a unanimous vote of the chapter for himself. Both sides therefore appealed to the Council, Raban in person, and Ulric through the advocacy of Nicholas. This was Nicholas's title to attend the Council, and for some months at least this appeal was his principal business there. He took the oaths, along with the Abbot of St. Matthias at Trèves and the Dean of

[1] Gregorovius, *Geschichte der Stadt Rom im Mittelalter*, vii, p. 34; Creighton, *History of the Papacy*, ii, pp. 196–7.
[2] Lenfant, *Histoire de la Guerre des Hussites et du Concile de Basle*, i, p. 330.

Wesel, as the three representatives of Ulric, on the 29th of February 1432. Thrice in the year he quitted the Council, when the cause did not require his presence. It has been pointed out that his attitude to the Pope began to change at the time when the Council finally gave a judgement unfavourable to Ulric.[1]

This participation in the larger affairs of the Council was connected in some considerable degree with his first book. This work, entitled *De concordantia catholica*, is devoted to an examination of the powers and prerogatives of General Councils and to the many other questions that arise from the consideration of that. The subject was uppermost in the minds of men at that time, and a work as bold and learned as the Cusan's was sure to make a considerable impression. The Church, he teaches, is a fraternity of believers, a living unity of souls in fellowship with Christ. An order of connexion is necessary, and this is provided by the hierarchy. In each diocese the Bishop represents and assures the unity of the Church; in the universal Church, the unity of the whole is assured and represented by the Pope. Because the primacy belongs to the see of Rome, it is the right of the Pope to summon a General Council, and it would not be a General Council if it did not include the Pope or his legate. But if the Pope dissociates himself, at a later stage, from a General Council properly assembled, the Council may continue its work for the good of the Church, though it should always treat the Pope with the utmost deference, and never decide, without him, upon dogmatic

[1] Vansteenberghe, *Nicolas de Cues*, p. 56.

questions. If, however, the Pope prove unfaithful, the Council must anathematize him, and withdraw from his obedience; in that case, the Pope is deposed.[1] For, as representing the universal Church, a General Council holds its authority immediately from Christ, and is therefore superior, both to the Pope personally, and to the Apostolic See.[2] The deposition of John XXIII and of Benedict XIII by the Council of Constance lent a great deal of weight to this contention. The schism was ended, and the whole Church rejoiced in the fact, and it was not to be denied that the end of the schism was due to the exercise, by a General Council, of its authority over rival Popes.

It is rather odd that Nicholas, in treating of the abuses of the Church, specially condemns pluralities. The *cumulus beneficiorum* was undoubtedly a great scandal, and played a great part in the movement for a reform of the Church, then and later. But Nicholas himself, at the time when he left the Council of Basel, when he was about thirty-seven years of age, was parish priest of Altrich, Canon of St. Simeon at Trèves, Canon of St. Mary at Oberwesel, Dean of St. Florin at Coblenz, and

[1] Gregory Heimburg did not forget these conclusions in later years in his invectives against Nicholas. ' If the Council of Constance had not deposed Pope John,' he wrote, ' Martin would not have succeeded to the Papal Chair, Eugenius would not have followed Martin, Nicholas would not have followed Eugenius, and then Nicholas could not have named thee Cardinal ! ' Scharpff, *Nicolaus von Cusa*, i, p. 339.

[2] Quare universaliter dici potest universale concilium, representationem catholicae Ecclesiae, habere potestatem immediate a Christo et esse omni respectu tam supra papam quam sedem apostolicam. *De concordantia catholica*, ii, 17, p. 736.

Provost of Münstermaifeld; and he had actually obtained, on the 13th of September 1427, a papal dispensation to allow him to hold some of these benefices which were incompatible by the law of the Church.[1]

Nicholas urges that civil society, if peace and prosperity are to be secured, must be organized on the ecclesiastical model, the lesser nobles corresponding to bishops, and the greater nobles to archbishops, the Kings answering to the Patriarchs, and the King of the Romans answering to the Pope. This passion for fanciful systematization is entirely characteristic of the Cusan; it appears again and again in his philosophy. So is the constant emphasis on harmony, *concordantia*.[2] Harmony results from order, from the due submission

---

[1] In later life he was a still more scandalous pluralist. In 1440 he received the benefice of Leye, in the diocese of Trèves, and in the same year he was allowed a reservation of six benefices in that diocese. The next year he was allowed to hold three benefices that were incompatible by the law of the Church. Five years later he was allowed to hold four benefices on the same terms. In 1442 he became Archdeacon of Brabant, and in 1446 he was dispensed from the obligation of residence in the archdeaconry. In 1462 he was given *in commendam* the Premonstratensian Abbey of St. Severin and St. Martin at Orvieto, and in 1463 he became Provost of St. Maurice at Hildesheim.

It is noticeable that three of Nicholas's relatives and friends succeeded to some of these benefices upon his death. John Römer became Provost at Hildesheim, Simon Wehlen became Provost at Münstermaifeld, and Peter Erkelenz received the living of Schindel, in the diocese of Liége. Vansteenberghe, *Nicolas de Cues*, pp. 86, 458.

[2] Gierke, *Das deutsche Genossenschaftsrecht*, iii, pp. 514–15. Gierke remarks that Dante bases his political theory in the *De Monarchia* (e.g. i, 7) on this order of ideas, and that the

of the parts and the unity of the whole. And it is on the perfect harmony of a double hierarchy, of the spiritual and of the temporal power, of the Church and of the Empire, that the welfare of religion and of humanity depends.[1] When this was the concluding theme of the work, it was appropriate that it should be dedicated to the principal representatives of the Church and of the Empire at the Council of Basel, Cardinal Cesarini and the Emperor Sigismund.[2] It was formally

De concordantia catholica of Nicholas is ' die letzte grossartige Fortbildung dieser Grundgedanken '.

For a high estimate of the practical value of Nicholas's proposals with regard to the organization of the Empire, see Janssen, *Geschichte des deutschen Volkes seit dem Ausgang des Mittelalters*, i, pp. 455–9. Nicholas's political doctrine is studied in an able essay entitled *Nicholas of Cusa*, by Dr. E. F. Jacob, in *The Social and Political Ideas of Some Great Thinkers of the Renaissance and the Reformation* (edited by F. J. C. Hearnshaw).

[1] See the last chapters of *De concordantia catholica*, iii, 40 and 41 (pp. 820–5).

[2] It is noticeable that Nicholas discredits the story of the Donation of Constantine, and a good deal else in the pseudo-Isidorian Decretals. *De concordantia catholica*, iii, 2, p. 782. He was the first to question the authenticity of the Decretals. Lorenzo Valla's attack on the Donation was a few years later.

We may note here another example of his historical insight. He suspected the authenticity of the pseudo-Dionysius. One of his manuscripts bears the note, in his own hand : Considera an loquatur (Athanasius) de Dionysio Areopagita sicut videtur ; et tunc mirum quod Ambrosius, Augustinus et Hieronymus ipsum Dionysium non viderunt, qui fuerunt post Athanasium. Damascenus etiam Dionysium allegat, qui fuit post illos, tempore saeculi VIII. Gregorius Papa ante Joh. Damascenum etiam Dionysium allegat. *Cod. cusan*, 44, f. i.

presented to the Council on the 7th of November
1433. In the assembly itself, as in the pages of the
Concordantia catholica, Nicholas was a bold and
eloquent advocate of the authority of the Council,
adopting much the same position as that of Gerson
at the Council of Constance seventeen years before.

Within a few weeks of the opening of the Council
of Basel, negotiations had been opened with the
Bohemians. The Pope had seized upon this as a
pretext to dissolve the Council, and on the 18th of
December he issued a Bull to that effect, summoning
another Council to meet within eighteen months
at Bologna. Cesarini wrote the Pope a daring
letter of protest.[1] It was unavailing, and he
declined the further presidency of the Council.
He remained at Basel, however, and became the
representative of a party of conciliation; late in
1432 he resumed the presidency. For the Council,
under the protection of the Emperor, refused to
dissolve, and entered upon a long and involved
dispute with the Pope. In April 1432, the Council
ordered the Pope to withdraw the Bull of dis-
solution, and to appear at Basel, in person or by
proxy, within three months. In June the Council
declared all the papal censures null and void, and
proceeded to appoint a governor of the papal
territory at Avignon.[2] In August the papal
plenipotentiaries appeared at Basel and argued the

---

[1] Cesarini's letter is a very remarkable document. See
Gieseler, *Ecclesiastical History*, iv, pp. 314–15, and Milman,
History of Latin Christianity, viii, pp. 348–50.

[2] It was rumoured at the Council that the Pope was about
to sell the fief of Avignon. Lenfant, *Histoire de la Guerre
des Hussites et du Concile de Basle*, ii, p. 69.

issue between the Pope and the Council. The
reply of the assembly, delivered on the 3rd of
September, was the definite declaration that a
General Council is superior to the Pope. On the
18th of December the Council gave the Pope a
further sixty days to withdraw his censures, and
on the 19th of February 1433, it solemnly declared
him contumacious. Before this, when it had been
decided to accuse the Pope of contumacy, Nicholas
had read a memoir on the procedure to be followed.
Six months later he was in a position of some
prominence. By the Bull *Dudum sacrum* of the
1st of August, the Pope had professed himself
ready to acknowledge the oecumenical character
of the Council, if it would annul the decrees already
passed infringing the prerogatives of the Papacy.
The reporters of the deputation *de Fide* were charged
to examine this document, which they did, and
reported unfavourably upon it. They were the
Bishop of Urbino, the Archdeacon of Metz, Jour-
dain Morin, and Nicholas of Cusa. The direct
result of their report was that the Council prepared
to suspend Eugenius, whereupon he yielded, and
on the 15th of December 1433, revoked his three
Bulls, and solemnly recognized the Council as the
supreme authority. Nicholas also prepared a manifesto, *De auctoritate praesidendi in concilio generale*,[1]
and spoke against Cesarini in the Council, on the
vexed question of the presidency. All this meant
that Nicholas had taken up an antipapal attitude
in a most definite way. Meanwhile he had lost
the cause that originally took him to Basel. On

[1] The text is in Duex, *Der deutsche Cardinal Nicolaus von
Cusa*, i, pp. 475–83.

the 15th of May the Council declared that the translation of Raban from Spires was canonical, and that he was really Archbishop of Trèves. Nicholas remained at Basel for some months, seeking to gain time by an appeal, since Ulric was still obstinate. But the cause was lost.

Nicholas passed the year 1435 at Münstermaifeld, where he had been elected Provost, on the nomination of Cesarini, and with the confirmation of the Council and the Pope.[1] He busied himself to secure some honourable compromise for Ulric. Finally Raban and Ulric accepted the arbitration of the Archbishop of Mainz, the Archbishop of Cologne, and the Bishop of Worms, who awarded Ulric a pension of 2,000 gold florins charged upon the revenue of the Archbishopric of Trèves, and the use of the castle of Stolzenfels. Nicholas returned to Basel early in 1436, and secured the assent of the Council to this arrangement. His attitude to the Council had changed in the interval, however. Ambrose Traversari had been writing letters to him for a year past, seeking to gain his allegiance for Eugenius IV, and it is clear that the correspondence had not been without result. For Nicholas now refused the position on the commission *de Fide*, to which he had been elected by the Council on the 2nd of March 1436, and declined henceforth to be a party to any new measures against the Pope.

Besides the *Concordantia catholica* and the small memoir *De auctoritate praesidendi in concilio generale*, there are two other writings of Nicholas, in connexion with the Council of Basel, that may be

[1] Rotta, *Il Cardinale Nicolò di Cusa*, p. 48.

noticed here—one relating to the Hussites, and one
to the reform of the calendar.

The Pope, in a Bull of the 1st of June 1431,
had proclaimed another crusade against the Bohemians, and had exhorted the estates of Germany
' to destroy the heretics utterly, and efface their
memory from the earth'. The result was the
disastrous defeat of the imperial army at Tauss, not
quite three months later. Cesarini, who had nar-
rowly escaped on that occasion, and who realized
the extreme seriousness of the position, addressed
an appeal to the Bohemians, in the interests of
peace, and the Council, recently assembled, invited
them to send representatives to Basel. The next
year a delegation from the Council met the Hussite
representatives at Eger, and, on the 18th of May,
signed with them a convention fixing the conditions of their sojourn at Basel. They arrived, led
by Procop and Rokyzana, on the 4th of January
1433. Nicholas was one of the theologians appointed by the Council to examine the points at
issue with the Bohemians, but he appears to have
confined himself, along with John of Ragusa, to
the question of communion in one or both kinds.
His conclusions are expressed in his *Epistolae ad
Bohemos*. In the first he argues the question of
authority, and urges that it is presumption to hold
to one's own opinion to the point of breaking the
unity of the Church. In the second he contends
that communion under two kinds cannot become
the source of any greater grace than that vouch-
safed through the single species.[1]

Besides writing the letters to the Bohemians,

[1] Duex, *Nicolaus von Cusa*, i, p. 142.

3

Nicholas played rather a prominent part in the negotiations with the representatives of Bohemia at the Council. As these negotiations were not going well, the Duke of Bavaria had a private consultation with Nicholas. On the 13th of March 1433, the latter, in the Duke's name, proposed that communion in both kinds should be allowed the Bohemians, on condition that they would yield upon the remainder of their four points, viz. the liberty of preaching, the sequestration of ecclesiastical property, and the punishment of mortal sin by the civil power. This effort did not meet with any immediate success. The Bohemian envoys declared that they were not armed with sufficient powers to accept a settlement, and they quitted Basel on the 14th of April, requesting the Council to send a deputation to Bohemia. There, at a later date, a settlement was achieved on the basis of the overtures of Nicholas. An agreement was signed at Prague on the 30th of November 1433, by John Rokyzana and the Calixtines, by which communion in two kinds was conceded, in the case of adults, on condition that the presence of the whole body of Christ under each species was formally recognized.[1]

The other of Nicholas's writings belonging to this period is of scientific rather than of theological interest. He presented his tract, *De reparatione Calendarii*, to the Council in 1437. The Council of

[1] Rotta, *Il Cardinale Nicolò di Cusa*, p. 173 ; Vansteenberghe, *Nicolas de Cues*, p. 216 ; Lutzow, *The Hussite Wars*, pp. 311, 361. A version of the text of the *Compactata* is in Lenfant, *Histoire de la Guerre des Hussites et du Concile de Basle*, ii, pp. 42-5.

Nicaea, in 325, had directed that Easter Sunday should be the Sunday following the full moon that happens upon, or next after, the vernal equinox, which was supposed to fall on the 21st of March. But through the inaccuracy of the Calendar the equinoxes were happening, apparently, too early, while Easter was being celebrated, actually, too late. The Julian Calendar held the solar year to be 365 days, 6 hours, which was 11 minutes 8 seconds too long. The Metonic cycle, by which the Western Church reckoned the age of the moon, presumed that the lunations corresponded exactly with the sun in the course of nineteen years, which involved an error of 1 hour 28 minutes 12 seconds in the cycle. The double error, as the years passed by, made the Calendars increasingly false.[1]

---

[1] 'The Julian rule made every fourth year, without exception, a bissextile. This is, in fact, an over-correction; it supposes the length of the tropical year to be 365¼ days, which is too great, and thereby induces an error of 7 days in 900 years. Accordingly, so early as the year 1414, it began to be perceived that the equinoxes were gradually creeping away from the 21st of March and September, where they ought always to have fallen had the Julian year been exact, and happening, as it appeared, too early. The necessity of a fresh and effectual reform in the Calendar was from that time continually urged, and at length admitted.' Sir John F. W. Herschel, *Outlines of Astronomy*, p. 638. But it is clear from a passage in Dante, *Paradiso*, xxvii, 142–3 :

> Ma prima che gennaio tutto si sverni
> Per la centesma ch'è laggiu negletta,

that this error and its consequences were familiar a century before the date named by Herschel.

And Roger Bacon was aware of the situation nearly fifty years before Dante wrote. He says that the Julian Calendar

Nicholas's tract first studies, with a wealth of mathematical and astronomical learning, the errors in the reckoning of the solar and lunar years, then proceeds to indicate the result of those errors, and finally urges the Council to adopt, without delay, a plan of reform. His remedy is to omit a week, and to change the 'golden number' into the 'golden circle'—the number of the lunar cycle. Thus in 1439 Whit-Sunday would fall on the 24th of May, and Nicholas's proposal is that that day should be reckoned as the 31st of May, and the 'golden circle' for that year should be 12, and for the next year 13 and so on. Thus the Calendar would be brought back to the rule of Nicaea, for one would only need to reckon forward from the new moon always found between the 8th of March and the 5th of April to find the date of Easter. To maintain the correctness of the Calendar henceforth, it would only be necessary to omit the extra day in leap year once every 304 years.

The Papal Legate appeared at Basel on the 3rd

made the solar year too long by $\frac{1}{130}$ of a day, and that the lunar cycle does not accurately correspond with nineteen years. He remarks that the inaccuracy of the Calendar led to grievous errors in keeping Easter, and that in 1267, the year in which he writes, Lent begins and ends a week too late. See the *Opus Majus*, (*Pars Quarta*) i, pp. 269–85 (Bridges' ed.).

In this matter Roger Bacon directly influenced Peter d'Ailly, who raised the question of the reform of the Calendar at the Council of Constance, and wrote a treatise upon it (of which there is an analysis in Lenfant, *Histoire de la Guerre des Hussites et du Concile de Basle*, i, pp. 695–700).

Nicholas once names Roger Bacon (*Excit.* vii, (*Medius vestrum*), p. 566), but the reference is on quite a minor point, and the Calendar is not mentioned.

of March 1437 and proposed the removal of the
Council to Florence or Udine. The pretext for
this was the prospect of negotiations with the
Greek Church. It could reasonably be urged
that the Byzantine representatives would dread the
journey across the Alps, and that some Italian
city, not too far from Venice, would be most
convenient for them. The Council rejected the
proposal, and proceeded to strong measures against
the Pope. On the 31st of July he was commanded
to appear at Basel. On the 18th of September the
Pope issued the Bull *Doctoris gentium*, in which he
threatened that unless the members of the Council
abandoned their rebellious attitude, and confined
themselves to the Bohemian affair, and that for a
limited period only, the Council would be transferred to Ferrara. The Council retaliated by
declaring the Bull to be null and void, and the
Pope himself guilty of contumacy. On the 30th
of December the Pope issued a Bull transferring
the Council to Ferrara. This was practically the
end of the Council of Basel. It continued to exist
and to fulminate for some years, but from this
point it ceased to have any considerable authority,
and here it need not concern us much more.

CHAPTER II

PAPAL ADVOCATE AND PAPAL LEGATE

FROM early in 1436, as we have seen, Nicholas had definitely abandoned his antipapal attitude in the Council of Basel. What was the secret of his change of front? Probably the turbulent conduct and the extreme measures of the Council itself. The voting by 'nations', which had been introduced at the Council of Constance, to reduce the power and preponderance of the Italian prelates, had been abolished, and now most of the danger was the other way. German and French clergy flooded the Council; they were near at hand, but it was a long and difficult journey for representatives from Italy and Spain and England. Moreover, the episcopal authority in the Council was lost. Decisions were carried by a tumultuous vote of all the members, whether learned or unlearned, whether dignitaries of the Church or the humblest clergy, or even laymen.[1] The lamentable account written by Aeneas Sylvius [2]

[1] Voigt, *Enea Silvio de' Piccolomini*, ii, p. 123.

[2] Aeneas Sylvius, *Comment.* (ed. Fea, Rome, 1823) p. 46; *Oratio adv. Australes* (in Muratori, *Anecdota*, ii, p. 162).

John of Palomar declared: Si Diabolus a Basileensibus aliquid peteret et contra fas et ius, dummodo illis vellet assentire facillime impetraret! In Mansi, *Sacrorum Conciliorum nova et amplissima collectio*, xxxi, p. 202.

is enough to show any one who is possessed of a little imagination why a philosophic mind would begin to despair, as the days passed, of any real reformation emerging from the clamorous democracy of the Council. Nicholas took the course which was taken a little later by Cesarini, whose motives have never been suspected.

Nicholas has been roundly accused of apostacy [1] for his desertion from the Council to the Pope, and it has been thought that the fact that he was named Cardinal *in petto* by Eugenius IV lends colour to the suggestion of unworthy motives. This is much less than fair to Nicholas. Obviously, on his whole record, he was an honest man. There was more than enough at Basel to disgust a sincere reformer, and he was that all his life long. His activities as Legate and as Bishop of Brixen are sufficient proof of it. [2] And the Cardinalate never came into view until he had rendered such service to Rome as no other man of his generation did or could. It was a reward that was natural enough for the services of the ten years preceding 1448, but it could scarcely have been foreseen as a possibility in 1437.

The question of the reunion of the Greek and Latin Churches undoubtedly influenced the attitude of Nicholas, and it had a considerable bearing upon the relations of the Pope and the Council. The initiative had been taken by Eugenius IV,

[1] See Voigt, *Enea Silvio de' Piccolomini*, iii, p. 310.
[2] See the *Reformatio generalis concepta per Reverendiss. D. Nicolaum de Cusa, Card. S. Petri ad Vincula*, in Scharpff, *Nicolaus von Cusa*, pp. 285–304; and Rotta, *Il Cardinale Nicolò di Cusa*, p. 202.

and Rome, Ancona, and Bologna had been mentioned as places suitable for the negotiations. The Council, in spite of the opposition of Cesarini, entered into separate negotiations with the Greeks, and proceeded to debate upon the place of meeting. The Patriarch and the Emperor demanded a maritime town, which was very natural, and insisted that it should be acceptable to the Pope. Avignon, Florence, and Basel itself were all suggested by partisans in the Council. Nicholas proposed to defer the decision, in the interests of peace, a course which Cesarini approved. Finally Nicholas voted for any place acceptable to the Pope and to the Greeks. Avignon was decided upon, but Cesarini refused to declare the vote, and the Pope refused to ratify it. This brought matters to a head. A month later, on the 7th of May 1437, the Cardinal of Arles read a decree convoking an assembly of Greeks and Latins at Basel, Avignon, or some town of Savoy. Cesarini read another naming Florence, Udine, or any other town which the Pope and the Greeks could agree upon. This, though the decision of the minority, was signed by the notaries, and (as the result of an audacious act) [1] bore the seal of the Council. Three of the leaders of the minority, the Bishop of Digne, the Bishop of Oporto, and Nicholas, left Basel on the 20th, carrying a copy of this decree, and letters from Cesarini to the Emperor and the Patriarch at Constantinople.

[1] This was a most extraordinary proceeding, and it is difficult to call it anything but a particularly daring fraud. The details are given by Valois, *Le Crise religieuse du XV⁰ siècle*, pp. 62–3.

When their mission had been approved by Eugenius IV at Bologna, they left Venice, in the papal galleys, about the middle of August, accompanied by the apostolic nuncios, the Archbishop of Tarentaise (the nephew of the Pope), and the Bishop of Coron.

It had been arranged that Constantinople should be guarded, during the absence of the Emperor, John Paleologus, by 300 Cretan arbalestiers. The Archbishop of Tarentaise and Nicholas disembarked at Candia to see to the equipment of this troop,[1] while their companions went on to Constantinople. When Nicholas and his comrade finally arrived in the Golden Horn, they saw the vessels in process of preparation to carry the Emperor and the Patriarch to Italy. Nicholas seems to have had a considerable share in overcoming the last hesitations of the Greeks. At sunset on the 27th of November 1437, the papal fleet, accompanied by the Greek triremes, set sail. They carried the Emperor, the Patriarch, and amongst a number of other prelates and monks, Bessarion, Archbishop of Nicaea, Mark, Archbishop of Ephesus, the Primate of Russia, the Bishops of Nicomedia, Heraclea, and Trebizond, the representatives of the Patriarchs of Alexandria, Antioch and Jerusalem, the Archimandrites of some of the greater monasteries, and the ecclesiast Syropolos, the future historian of the Council.[2] The voyage was long and difficult. On the 8th of February 1438, the fleet arrived at the Lido, and was met by the Bucentaur, and many galleys and

---

[1] Scharpff, *Nicholas von Cusa*, p. 113.
[2] Syropolos, *Vera historia*, ii, 21, p. 17.

gondolas, bearing the Doge and the Senate of
Venice in their robes of purple silk. When the
fleet reached the Piazza of St. Mark it was received
with salutes of artillery, fanfares of trumpets, and
the ringing of all the bells in Venice. Nicholas
and the Bishop of Digne hurried on to Ferrara to
report to the Pope.

The Council which was to bring about the
pretence of a union between the Greek and the
Roman Churches was opened by Eugenius IV in the
Church of St. George, without the Porta Romana.
Technically, from the papal point of view, it was
the Council of Basel which had been transferred
to Ferrara,[1] and presently those who remained at
Basel were excommunicated. The Council was
shortly afterward transferred to Florence, mainly,
it would seem, because the condottiere Niccolo
Piccinino was rendering the neighbourhood of
Ferrara unsafe.[2]

The Emperor Sigismund took occasion of the
decree of suspension passed upon Eugenius IV
by the Council of Basel to break off relations with
the Council and to rally to the Pope, especially
in support of the attempt to reunite the Western

[1] There were communications, however, between the
Greeks and the Council at Basel, and it is possible that
Nicholas had some part in these. The document containing the reply of Mark of Ephesus and Bessarion of Nicaea
to the statement of the Latin doctrine of purgatory drawn
up by Cesarini is said to have been delivered to the Council
of Basel by Nicholas, *praesentata Nicolao Cusano*. See *Patrologia Orientalis*, (ed. Graffin and Nau) xv, *fasc.* 1, p. 8.

[2] Gregorovius, *Geschichte der Stadt Rom im Mittelalter*, iii,
p. 69. Syropolos remarks (*Vera historia*, vii, 12, p. 205)
ἑάλωσαν καὶ δύο πόλεις αὐτῶν παρὰ τοῦ Νικολὸ Πιζζινή.

and Eastern Churches. But the Electoral Princes of Germany, met at Frankfort on the 17th of March 1438, solemnly decided on neutrality as between the Pope and the Council. For the next few years the Pope, on the one hand, and the Council, on the other, did their best to turn the German neutrality to their own profit. This determined the activities of Nicholas for practically the whole of the period. He did more than any other man to maintain and increase the hold of the Papacy upon his native land, and he entirely deserved the name which Aeneas Sylvius bestowed upon him, when he called Nicholas ' the Hercules of the Eugenians '.[1]

In October 1438, along with Cardinal Albergati and the Archbishop of Tarentaise, the papal nuncios, John of Torquemada and Nicholas of Cusa attended the Diet of Nuremberg, where they opposed the representatives of the Council. Some months later the Patriarch of Aquileia, the legate from Basel, visited Mainz, and was given a splendid reception. Before a great assembly in the Cathedral Nicholas raised his voice in defence of the Pope. He had no official mission on this occasion, and he was expelled. He went about the city all the more, however, discrediting the mission of the delegates from Basel, until they themselves sought to meet him in discussion. Finally Nicholas was authorized to take part in the deliberations of the Diet, and therefore secured the right and the

[1] Hercules tamen omnium Eugenianorum Nicolaus Cusanus existimatus est, homo et priscarum literarum eruditissimus et multarum rerum usu perdoctus. Aeneas Sylvius, *De rebus gestis bas. Concil.* See *Opera* (Basel, 1571), p. 3.

opportunity to defend the Pope. He could also keep Cesarini and the Pope himself acquainted with what happened in the Diet.

Upon the arrival of the news that the Council, on the 25th of March, had declared the Pope a heretic, many of those present at the Diet went to Basel, and Nicholas went also. He seems to have been present on the 25th of June, when the Council proceeded to the last extremity, and the Bishop of Marseilles read the decree pronouncing the deposition of Eugenius IV. The immediate result was a reaction of feeling in favour of the Pope. Ten days later, on the 5th of July, the union of the Latin and Greek Churches [1] was proclaimed at Florence, in the Duomo, and this striking fact still further exalted the papal prestige. It did not appear until later how slight and delusive the union really was. Nicholas hailed it as setting the seal of a supernatural approval upon the action of the Pope, as against that of the Council. ' The work of the Holy Spirit ', said he, ' is unity and peace : it is at Florence and not at Basel, that He has breathed upon the Fathers ! ' Eugenius, as was natural, rejoiced exceedingly. ' Shout, O heavens, and exult, O earth ! ' (he wrote). ' The wall of partition that divided the Eastern from the Western Church has fallen ! . . . All the faithful throughout the wide earth, all who call themselves by the name of Christ, may bring felicitations to their Mother, the Catholic Church, and may rejoice with her ! '

A little later and the fortunes of the Papal party

---

[1] The decree of union was drawn up by Nicholas's friend, Ambrose Traversari.

ebbed again. On the 5th of November the Council of Basel elected Amadeus of Savoy as Pope, and after some hesitation he accepted the tiara and took the name of Felix V. He was acknowledged by two great religious Orders, the Carthusians and the Teutonic Knights, by the Universities of Vienna, Erfurt, Cologne, Leipzig and Cracow, by the Duke of Bavaria and the Markgraf of Brandenburg, and by many Archbishops and Bishops. This complicated the situation, and affected the propaganda of Nicholas. It was now his effort to win the princes and the people of Germany over to the obedience of Eugenius, not from a position of neutrality merely, but, in the case of some of them, from allegiance to the anti-Pope. He pleaded this cause, with a good deal of applause and success, at the Diet held at Mainz, in March 1441,[1] and at another held at Frankfort, in June 1442,[2] and undoubtedly won over a great many to the side of Eugenius, besides generally shaking the credit of the partisans of Basel and Felix V. It was also largely due to the influence of Nicholas, though still more to that of Aeneas Sylvius, that the Diet of Frankfort in September 1446 adopted an attitude which led finally, six months later, to the Emperor Frederick III and the Electors of Magdeburg and Brandenburg making their submission to Eugenius IV.

On the 23rd of February 1447, Eugenius died. After a pontificate of many vicissitudes, he lived barely long enough to see the Papacy restored to

---

[1] Scharpff, *Reformator*, p. 133; Creighton, *History of the Papacy*, iii, p. 29.

[2] Scharpff, *Reformator*, ii, p. 135.

power and prestige. Almost his last official act was to receive the envoys who gave the declaration of the Emperor's fidelity.

It was expected that Eugenius would be succeeded by Prospero Colonna, the nephew of Martin V. On the first scrutiny he had ten votes, and Capranica eight. In the hope that the partisans of these two candidates might be brought to agree upon the choice of a third, several names of men outside the College were suggested, including those of the Archbishop of Benevento and Nicholas of Cusa. Finally Thomas Parentucelli was elected and took the style of Nicholas V. He was a man of considerable ability and learning. He was the patron of scholars like Laurentius Valla, Poggio Bracciolini, Bessarion, and George of Trebizond, and may be said to be the first Pope who fostered the Renaissance.

Nicholas of Cusa and his colleague Carvajal appeared for the last time as the papal representatives at Aschaffenburg in July 1447, when the Electors of Cologne, of Trèves, of Saxony, and of the Palatinate abandoned the cause of Felix, and gave in their allegiance to the successor of Eugenius. The next month an imperial edict declared the abolition of German neutrality, and the adhesion of the Empire to Rome. Poland and Aragon had already submitted. In 1448 France was restored to the Roman obedience. The same year Felix V resigned, the Council of Basel was dissolved, and the schism was at an end. It was a victory for the Papacy, in which Nicholas of Cusa could claim a considerable share. He had largely won Germany [1]

[1] Vansteenberghe, *Nicolas de Cues*, p. 85.

to the side of the Pope at Rome, and the adhesion of Germany to the one side or the other in the long dispute between Basel and Rome, and latterly in the rivalry between Pope and anti-Pope, was certainly the deciding factor. Eugenius had not been ungrateful for the undoubted services of Nicholas. He made him Archdeacon of Brabant, and dispensed him from residence in the diocese; he gave him about a dozen different benefices, mostly in the bishoprics of Trèves and Liége, and authorized him to hold those which were incompatible, and finally he named him Cardinal *in petto*, probably on the 16th of December 1446.[1] His actual promotion to the office was due to Nicholas V. He was included in the list of promotions to the Cardinalate on the 20th of December 1448, and he was given the title of San Pietro in Vincoli on the 3rd of January 1449.[2] He did not arrive in Rome until a year later, on the 11th of January 1450, when his colleagues conducted him the same day to the papal palace, and he received the red hat. His elevation to the Cardinalate made a great impression in Germany.

[1] The day when Carvajal was also named Cardinal. Uebinger, *Zur Lebensgeschichte des Nikolaus Cusanus* in *Historisches Jahrbuch des Görres-Gesellschaft*, xiv, p. 552.

[2] Scharpff, *Nicolaus von Cusa*, p. 152. The autobiographical manuscript (in Uebinger, *Lebensgeschichte*, p. 550, and in Marx, *Stiftungen*, p. 221) states: Hic dominus Nicolaus (fuit) per papam Eugenium in cardinalem assumptus secrete: et statim mortuo Eugenio ante eis publicationem fuit iterum per Nicolaum papam quintum in presbyterum cardinalem tituli sancti Petri ad vincula assumptus et publicatus anno domini 1449 in proxima angaria post diem cinerum, quo anno Amadeus antipapa cessit nomini papatus. *Historia Reverendissimi Domini Cardinalis Nicolai de Cusa.*

A German Cardinal was a portent, *monstrum corvo rarius albo*, as it was said.[1] Nicholas was often called *Cardinalis Teutonicus*. Six weeks later Johannes Röttel, the Bishop of Brixen, died, and the Pope appointed the new Cardinal to the vacant see. He received episcopal consecration from the hands of the Pope himself, on the 23rd of March.[2]

It had been the steady policy, for two generations, of the Archdukes of Austria, as Counts of the Tyrol, to enlarge their frontiers at the expense of the neighbouring bishoprics of Trent, Chur, and Brixen, which were ecclesiastical principalities directly subject, in temporal matters, to the Emperor. Frederick, the father of the reigning Count Sigismund, had compelled the Bishop of Brixen and the Bishop of Trent to acknowledge his temporal sovereignty.[3] Later he wished to force them into making common cause with him against the King of the Romans, and the Bishop of Brixen had agreed to do so ; the Bishop of Trent had refused, and the Duke had retaliated by a military occupation of his diocese. This was the situation when Sigismund succeeded his father in 1446. It was his desire to force the complete secularization of the two bishoprics. The next Bishop of Trent was a mere creature of the Duke's : Sigismund compelled the two candidates, one elected by the Chapter, and the other nominated by Eugenius IV, to renounce their pretensions to the see, and put forward another candidate of his own, who was

[1] Duex, *Nicolaus von Cusa*, ii, p. 2.
[2] Scharpff, *Nicolaus von Cusa*, p. 153.
[3] Vansteenberghe, *Nicolas de Cues*, p. 167.

recognized, on the 17th of October 1446, by the Council of Basel. He had even less trouble with Brixen, when that see fell vacant, for the Chapter elected a Bishop, recognized by the anti-Pope Felix V, who readily accepted the conditions which had been forced upon his predecessor, and, in addition, raised troops for the Duke, put the strong places in his diocese at the Duke's service, and became the Duke's chancellor.

On his death in 1450, the Chapter elected, through three delegates, Leonard Wiesmayer, who was also attached to the court of the Duke, as privy councillor and chancellor,[1] and he, without waiting for confirmation from Rome, promptly took possession of the see. The election was certainly not canonical; a Bull of Nicholas V states expressly that it was the act of the canons when locked up in a residence of the Duke's, and surrounded by armed men, and that ' the violence of the Duke rendered a free election impossible '. The Pope's action in appointing Nicholas of Cusa to the see could probably be justified on this ground alone, but he seems to have been well within his rights on other grounds as well. The Concordat of Vienna, in 1448, provided that the Pope could appoint another person as Bishop, even when the election had been canonical, if he judged, on reasonable and manifest grounds, and after consultation with the Cardinals, that his nominee was a person of greater worth, who could render greater service in the position. If ever there was an occasion on which the Pope

[1] Marx, *Stiftungen*, p. 158; Jaeger, *Der Streit des Cardinals Nicolaus von Cusa mit dem Herzoge Sigmund von Oesterreich*, i, p. 6.

4

was warranted in exercising this discretion, this was one. The whole history of the relations between the Bishops of Brixen and the Archdukes of Austria for a generation past justified the papal action.

Sigismund and the Chapter naturally opposed the appointment of Nicholas, and persisted in their opposition, though counselled to submit by the Archbishop of Trèves, who had been asked to intervene in favour of the elected candidate. The Pope threatened the ducal territories with an interdict. This was twice postponed at the request of Nicholas, and meantime both parties were active. The Pope sent Carvajal, the old comrade of Nicholas in the legation, to explain his action to the chapter of Brixen, and the Duke summoned representatives of the nobility and of the citizens of the Tyrol to Sterzing, to prepare for resistance.

By a Bull of the 31st of October 1450, the Pope ratified the appointment of Nicholas, denounced the rebellious attitude of the Duke, and demanded the support of the faithful. Nicholas traversed the diocese in January 1451, in setting out on his work as Legate, and possibly met the Duke and the Chapter. He was scarcely out of the territory of the Bishopric, however, when the Chapter declared his nomination null and void, and appealed to the Pope better informed, or to the next General Council. The matter was settled in a singular way. Eugenius IV, in February 1446, had accorded to the King of the Romans the privilege of naming and presenting a candidate for the Bishoprics of Brixen, Trent, and some other sees, and the privilege had been later confirmed in a Bull of Nicholas V.

It occurred to Nicholas of Cusa to have recourse to this royal prerogative. He presented himself before Frederick III, at Wiener-Neustadt, on the 1st of March 1451, and Frederick, apparently without making any difficulty, recognized him as Bishop of Brixen, and confirmed him in the possession of all the episcopal rights and privileges.[1] Armed with this royal approval Nicholas presented himself at the assembly which was convoked at Salzburg, by the Archbishop, at the request of the Pope, on the 15th of March, with the purpose of settling the whole dispute. There were present the Archbishop and his suffragan, the Bishop of Chiemsee, Nicholas of Cusa, Leonard Wiesmayer, the Provost of the Chapter and three canons, and two jurists representing the Duke. A settlement was effected. Wiesmayer resigned his claim, on the promise of suitable compensation; the Chapter rendered obedience to Nicholas, and he promised them, without reserve, that they should elect his successor. The relations of the Bishop and the Duke were settled in very vague terms. For a year after this there was peace between the Duke and the absent Bishop. In the Jubilee year of 1450, the new Pope, Nicholas V, decided to send out Legates *a latere* to various countries in Europe, and designated Nicholas of Cusa as Legate for Germany, Bohemia and the neighbouring lands.[2] In the Bull of the 29th of December 1450, the Pope emphasizes the qualifications of the Cardinal—his

[1] Jaeger, *Der Streit*, i, p. 33.
[2] Uebinger, *Kardinallegat Nikolaus Cusanus in Deutschland*, in *Historisches Jahrbuch der Görres-Gesellschaft*, viii (1887). p. 650.

knowledge, his experience, his zeal, and especially his perfect knowledge of the German language. The Legate was charged to proclaim the Jubilee, and to offer indulgences to those who had not been able to visit Rome during the privileged season; he was authorized to hold local and provincial councils, and to preside over these in the name of the Pope, to visit and reform monasteries, to regulate pluralities, and to absolve in cases reserved to the Holy See. In order that his mission of reform might not be hindered, all special privileges of clergy and churches were suspended before the Legate, except those of Bishops and Archbishops. He was also allowed, in case of need, to appeal to the secular arm.

Nicholas began his journey on the last day of the year 1450. He had a retinue of thirty persons, which seems to have been a much more modest equipage than Cardinal-Legates were accustomed to exhibit. Nevertheless, his arrival at a city and his departure from it were often like a royal progress. The clergy and the religious Orders went in procession to meet him, dukes and bishops greeted him on his entry into their domains, and escorted him to the border of the next diocese, or the next principality. The wealthy towns of the Low Countries gave him splendid hospitality at their stately *hôtels de ville* during his stay.

The proclamation of the indulgence was one principal part of the Legate's duties. He published this at Salzburg, on the 8th of February 1451, for Austria, Styria, Carinthia, and the Tyrol; at Nuremberg on the 18th of April, for the territories of the Duke of Bavaria; at Magdeburg, on the

19th of June, for Brandenburg, Saxony, Posen, and Pomerania; at Hildesheim, on the 6th of July, for Brunswick and Luneburg, and at the same place, on the 12th of July, for the diocese of Hildesheim; at Minden on the 5th of August, for Silesia; at Utrecht, on the 17th of September, for Holland, Zeeland, and Frisia; at Nimuegen, about the 23rd of September, and at Ruremonde, on the 26th, for the Duchy of Gueldres; at Aix-la-Chapelle, a few days later, for the city and its environs; then at Maestricht for the territories of Fauquemont, Daehlen, and Limburg; and finally, at Tongres and at Hasselt, on the 11th of October.[1]

This list provides the barest sketch of Nicholas's travels during the year. Besides the places named, he visited Munich, Ratisbon, Bamberg, Würzburg, Erfurt, Halle, Hanover, Amsterdam, Haarlem, Leyden, Delft, Cologne, Mainz, and Trèves (with an excursion to his native village of Cues), and many other towns of less importance. Everywhere he preached, held assemblies of the clergy, inquired into abuses, confirmed or cancelled ecclesiastical privileges, summoned delinquents to judgement, issued decrees, wrote letters, interviewed visitors, and generally seems to have done sincere and strenuous service as an ecclesiastical reformer.[2]

A spirit of hostility manifested itself here and there, in respect of the indulgence. There was a widespread feeling that the whole business was merely a pretext to raise money. At various places the clergy seized part of the money, and refused

---

[1] Vansteenberghe, *Nicolas de Cues*, p. 94.
[2] Scharpff, *Nicolaus von Cusa*, pp. 140–1.

to give it up, and Nicholas had to threaten the culprits with excommunication, the loss of their benefices, and even an appeal to the secular arm.

It is interesting to notice that in the course of his reforming activities Nicholas took a strong line against several of the superstitious cults of the time, such as the devotion paid to certain 'bloody Hosts', particularly that of Wilsnack.[1] About seventy years before, this Brandenburg village had been burned down, and it was said that amid the blackened ruins of the church, the altar had been discovered intact, with three Hosts covered with blood. These were preserved in a crystal reliquary, and soon became an object of devotion. It was said that miraculous cures were wrought through their agency, and a pilgrimage to the shrine was speedily established, which was favoured by the local bishops, and granted special indulgences by Urban IV. Crowds of pilgrims came from every part of Germany and Flanders, and even from England and Scandinavia, to the 'Holy Blood of Wilsnack', and the result was that a new and splendid church was built, and that the village grew into a town.

---

[1] Scharpff, *Nicolaus von Cusa*, p. 165 ; Rotta, *Il Cardinale Nicolò di Cusa*, p. 84. The Holy Blood of Wilsnack had long been a scandal. A generation earlier than this, the Archbishop of Prague had appointed a commission to investigate gross frauds in connexion with it. John Hus was a member of this commission, and he gives an account of the superstition in his treatise *De omni sanguine Christi glorificato*. *Opera*, i, pp. 158–62. See Loserth, *Wiclif and Hus*, pp. 102–3, and Workman, *The Dawn of the Reformation*, pp. 131–2. There were many instances of this peculiarly gross superstition in the Middle Ages.

There were those, however, who were opposed to the devotion, and the matter was raised at the Synod of Magdeburg, and discussed in the presence of Nicholas. The University of Erfurt was consulted, and there was much controversy about the case. Nicholas pronounced adverse judgement in a decree issued at Halberstadt on the 5th of July 1451. He wrote: 'The faithful take the red colour of the Hosts for the blood of Christ, and the priests not merely tolerate, but actually encourage that belief, because of the money that it brings to them. . . . We cannot but protest against this. The Catholic Faith assures us that the glorified body of Christ has a glorified blood, which is completely invisible. It is necessary to remove from the people all occasion of error. We therefore command that wherever in the territory of our legation there exist such transformed Hosts, the priests shall not exhibit them, nor speak of miracles in connexion with them, nor allow leaden images to be made with their likeness. These Hosts are to be consumed by a celebrant, rather than that the Eucharist should disappear by corruption of species.'

The decree failed in its purpose. The Bishop of Havelburg withstood his metropolitan, faced both excommunication and an interdict, and won the day. Pope Nicholas V was constrained to authorize the pilgrimage afresh, on condition that a recently consecrated Host was exposed to the veneration of the faithful along with the 'bloody Hosts'. The Holy See gave fresh indulgences to the pilgrimage in 1471, and again in 1500, and it was not until the Reformation that the cult ceased, when, in 1552, the then incumbent of Wilsnack burnt the famous Hosts.

One of the principal objects of Nicholas's mission was the reformation of the lives of the clergy and the monks. There was ample need for this. Nicholas attempted to bring about a better state of affairs, in the first place, by holding provincial councils. There was a double advantage in this. The Cardinal personally encountered the dignitaries who would be charged with the execution of these decrees, and the decrees themselves acquired a more local authority and a more democratic sanction than if they had been merely the orders of a Legate representing the Pope and the curia.

The enormous territory of the legation comprised the ecclesiastical provinces of Salzburg, Mainz, Magdeburg, Cologne, and Trèves. Nicholas held a provincial council at Salzburg on the 3rd of February 1451, at Magdeburg on the 20th of June, at Mainz on the 14th of November,[1] and at Cologne on the 23rd of February 1453.[2] The principal evils against which these provincial councils legislated were simony and concubinage. Both were widely prevalent. Simony had grown into a system, largely through the avarice of monasteries and collegiate foundations which extorted heavy payments from those appointed to benefices in their gift, and very often exacted a preliminary oath from the beneficiary, to make the payments secure. Concubinage was not only widespread,

[1] For the decrees, see Scharpff, *Reformator*, p. 185.
[2] Uebinger, *Kardinallegat Nikolaus Cusanus in Deutschland*, in *Historisches Jahrbuch der Görres-Gesellschaft*, viii (1887), p. 665.

but in many places it was practised quite openly, and with the frank approval of the laity. The fact is that the celibacy of the clergy had never been rigidly enforced, and despite the measures of Hildebrand, the marriage of priests had continued. Often concubinage seems to have been regarded as a species of marriage which was valid despite some canonical irregularity. In any case clerical concubinage was a general and a recognized practice. Under the pretext of attacking it, prelates often made it a regular source of revenue.[1] They imposed fines on priests who had concubines, which the priests paid, and then were troubled no more. The right of *collagium*, in fact, was a practice by which priests purchased a dispensation from celibacy and the right to keep a concubine.[2]

The reform of the monasteries came only second to that of the parochial clergy. Many of the monks, according to Nicholas's own words, 'disobeyed their rules, had evil habits, and lived a dissolute life'. The Archbishops and Bishops were charged to warn the monks of each religious house that if the life of their monastery were not regularized within a year, the monastery would be deprived of all privileges, and the monks themselves would become incapable of all ecclesiastical dignities or employment. In addition to these general provisions there were special regulations for the Cistercians, the Benedictines, and the Augustinians. There was considerable opposition

---

[1] Lindsay, *History of the Reformation*, ii, p. 486 (and the extract from the *Rolls of Parliament*, ii, pp. 313–14 given there).

[2] Lagarde, *The Latin Church in the Middle Ages*, p. 408.

to all these reforming efforts. At Augsburg and at Deddingen, for example, the visitors of the monasteries were attacked and imprisoned; at Nuremberg it came to fighting with daggers; and the Landgraf of Hesse was actually poisoned by refractory monks whom he was trying to reform.

A Diet was held at Vienna late in 1452, to compose a dispute which had arisen in consequence of Ladislas of Bohemia having been placed under the tutelage of the Emperor Frederick III.[1] Frederick asked the Pope to send a Legate, and he sent Nicholas of Cusa and the Bishop of Siena, better known as Aeneas Sylvius. Nicholas sought to use the occasion of the Diet for another attempt at reconciliation with the Bohemians, but he was discouraged by the attitude of Ludwig and Otto of Bavaria, and of Ladislas, and nothing came of it.

There was some intention at this time of sending Nicholas as Legate to England,[2] with the purpose of establishing peace between this country and France. The Pope had been urged to do this by the Duke of Burgundy. The Cardinal d'Estouteville was sent, however, and Nicholas never landed on these shores.

---

[1] Creighton, *History of the Papacy*, ii, p. 302; Jaeger, *Der Streit*, i, p. 75.

[2] Scharpff, *Nicolaus von Cusa*, pp. 195–6. Marx apparently believes that Nicholas came to England in 1451, but he does not quote any specific evidence. See the Introduction to *Verzeichnis der Handschriften-Sammlung des Hospitals zu Cues*. There seems to be no possible time in that year for a visit to these shores, in the light of Nicholas's itinerary as printed by Vansteenberghe, *Nicolas de Cues*, pp. 483–9. See Rotta, *Il Cardinale Nicolò di Cusa*, p. 103.

CHAPTER III

BISHOP OF BRIXEN

NICHOLAS had now finished his work as Legate, and he turned his thoughts to his own diocese of Brixen, among the mountains of the Tyrol, in the domain of the Archduke Sigismund of Austria. The House of Austria held the largest territories in Germany at this time (for much of the Luxemburg heritage lay outside Germany proper). The Austrian duchies had been kept together, under the joint administration of brothers, until a family quarrel in 1411 ended in the separation of Austria from the other duchies of Carinthia and the Tyrol. Albert, who later became the son-in-law and successor of the Emperor Sigismund, ruled Austria; Ernest, his cousin, ruled Carinthia, Styria, and Carniola; and the Tyrol fell to Frederick, another cousin. The latter died in 1439, and was succeeded by Sigismund, who reigned until 1492. The title of Archduke was conferred on the whole family by the Emperor Frederick III. It was this Archduke Sigismund with whom Nicholas waged the great struggle of his life.

In the middle of March 1452, the Cardinal left Coblenz, and the banks of the Moselle, which he was never to see again, and took the road to the Alps. He entered upon possession of the diocese at Easter 1452. The bishopric was suffragan of the archbishopric of Salzburg. The decrees of the provincial council, which Nicholas had held at Salzburg in February 1451, were therefore binding upon the diocese of Brixen. There was much need for them to be rigorously applied. Crime and concubinage were frequent, and the decrees of the Council of Basel upon the latter subject had been almost without effect.

Nicholas summoned a diocesan synod for the month of February 1453, and subsequent synods were held in 1455 and 1457. It had been his intention to hold a yearly synod, but that plainly proved impossible. The diocese was a mountainous region, where roads were scarce and bad, and most of the priests were scattered in remote villages, high among the hills, and difficult of access. The synod of 1453 renewed the decree against concubinage, and gave the guilty parties a month to reform their lives, under the penalty of being deprived of their benefices, and expelled from the diocese. A series of detailed enactments followed, which prescribed almost every point of duty and behaviour in a priest's life. The clergy are not to frequent taverns, or to play at cards or dice. They are not to wear long hair or large hats, rings or jewels, garments of striking colours, or of ultra-fashionable cut.[1] They are to instruct the people in the faith, teaching them the meaning of the sacraments and of the Commandments, and reciting the Paternoster with them, urging them to come

---

[1] The account of clerical dress and behaviour given in Dr. Carl Schmidt's *Johannes Tauler von Strassburg*, pp. 41-2, shows the necessity for such regulations, the sumptuary ones among the rest.

to Mass fasting, and forbidding the sale of victuals before the end of Mass. They are to guard the people against superstition, forbidding pilgrimages except those to Brixen, to Rome, to St. James of Compostella, or others which have been long established; suppressing all books of prayers or exorcisms not recognized by the Church, and generally discouraging sortilege and incantations.[1] The clergy of the dioceses are divided into three chapters, which are to meet yearly; each chapter is to possess a standard missal agreeing with the text of that possessed by the episcopal vicar, and copies of the diocesan statutes, of the *De fide et sacramentis* of St. Thomas Aquinas, and of the *Summa* of John of Auerbach.[2]

The priests were forbidden to preach to the people about 'superstitious matters', such as those found in the lives of St. Blaise, St. Barbe, St. Catharine, St. Dorothy, and other saints in the *Golden Legend*.[3] The celebration of certain feasts

[1] Compare the passage in one of his sermons, *Excit.*, ii (*Ibant Magi*), p. 391.

[2] None of the authorities upon Nicholas's life give any information whatever as to this writer or his book. He seems to have been a contemporary of the Cardinal's, or nearly so. He wrote a *Directorium curatorum*, and a *Summa de sacramentis*—the latter is evidently the book referred to in the text. The title-page describes him as *Vicarius Bambergensis*. The other book describes him as *Decretorum Doctor*. The *Summa* was printed at Augsburg in 1469.

[3] For these saints, see de Douhet, *Dictionnaire des Légendes du Christianisme*, pp. 56–9 (St. Barbe); pp. 273–5 (St. Blaise); pp. 282–7 (St. Catharine); pp. 1166–9 (St. Dorothy, i.e. St. Theodora). The references in the *Legenda aurea* (Leipzig, 1850) are pp. 898, 167, 791. Nicholas attacked the cult of St. Blaise again in *Excit.*, ii (*Ibant Magi*), p. 391.

was forbidden since they had arisen 'from superstition rather than from worship', such as the Octave of the Epiphany, the feast of St. Valentine, and offices said for the purpose of averting storms, epilepsy, cattle plague, and so forth. Two years later, at the Synod of 1457, Nicholas had to reaffirm his ordinances with regard to the correction of the service books, and the annual Chapters of the clergy. The Chapters were to be held henceforth at a fixed date, at Brixen, Innichen, and Wilten, each under the presidency of a canon, who is named, and whose duty it would be to present a faithful report to the ensuing diocesan synod.

It is obvious that Nicholas was meeting with a good deal of apathy, in his efforts to reform his diocese. He was to meet with more than apathy henceforth; he was to encounter active resistance and bitter hostility. It is significant that this was more from the religious Orders than from the parish priests, though there was disaffection enough among these. Upon his entry into the diocese he had posted on the doors of the Cathedral at Brixen the decree issued at Salzburg with regard to the reform of the monasteries, and the ordinance as to the strict enclosure of nuns.[1] Twelve months later, there were six religious houses in the diocese which had taken no account whatever of the decree. On a visit to Rome after the Synod of 1453, Nicholas had been given by the Pope a special mission to visit and reform the monasteries of his diocese with the title of Legate. He had authority to

---

[1] Jaeger, *Der Streit*, i, p. 60.
[2] Vansteenberghe, *Nicolas de Cues*, p. 143.

punish and deprive of office all who were refractory, and to bestow special privileges upon the monasteries which spontaneously submitted themselves to the policy of reformation.

The greatest difficulty encountered by Nicholas in his mission of monastic reform was at Sonnenburg,[1] and this led directly to all the later troubles which clouded his career as Bishop of Brixen.[2] The convent had been founded in 1018. The ruins of it may still be seen, overlooking the valley of the Rienz. The nuns were recruited from the daughters of the Tyrolese nobility, and they seem to have lived in the grossest laxity. The convent had been originally placed under the protection of the Bishop of Trent, but it had gradually extended its jurisdiction over the valleys of Enneberg, Wengen, and Abtei. This led to a dispute with the Bishop of Brixen, which was concluded in 1447, five years before Nicholas entered his diocese, and three before he was appointed Bishop, by an agreement which recognized the Bishop's authority over these valleys for ten years to come. Subsequently to this agreement, the convent had forced a quarrel upon the peasants of the valley of Enneberg, as to the rights of pasturage on the Grünwald, which they had possessed unchallenged for generations. The Abbess, Verena Stuben, complained to Sigismund, the

[1] There had been strife between the Bishops of Brixen and the cloister of Sonnenburg as early as 1382. Jaeger, *Der Streit*, i, p. 48.

[2] For the whole quarrel between Nicholas and Sigismund, see the monograph of Jaeger, *Der Streit des Cardinals Nicolaus von Cusa mit dem Herzoge Sigmund von Oesterreich*.

Duke, who upheld the nuns, and condemned the peasants. The latter appealed to the Bishop of Brixen. Upon the arrival of Nicholas, the Duke cited the opposing parties to appear before him. Nicholas forthwith forbade the Abbess to obey the summons, on the ground that, as Bishop, he was the rightful court of appeal for the nuns, as well as for the peasants. The Duke advised the Abbess to resist, whereupon the Cardinal invited her to remit the cause to him, if not as the Bishop, at least as the Legate of the Pope. She professed to accept, but appealed to the Duke for help, and he declared that he was not prepared to forgo his sovereign rights. The Bishop then summoned the Abbess to observe the convention of 1447, in default of which he should take such action as seemed good to him, whereupon Sigismund, to forestall the episcopal action, summoned the peasants to appear on the 24th of June 1453.

A month before this date, Nicholas had ordered the decree of the 2nd of May 1452, with regard to the strict enclosure of nuns, to be affixed to the gates of Sonnenburg.[1] The Abbess promised to obey, while at the same time appealing to the Duke to rule that the reforms were not to be carried out, except by agreement. Then, profiting by the delay which Nicholas granted, on account of his absence at the Diet of Ratisbon, the Abbess published a protest against the reforms, which were declared to be dictated by hate, and intended to hamper the convent in the dispute with the peasants of Enneberg. This rebellious manifesto concluded by threatening an appeal to the Holy See, and placing

[1] Jaeger, *Der Streit*, i, p. 65.

the convent under the protection of the Duke. The Duke in turn assigned the pasturage of the Grünwald to the convent, informed Nicholas that as the protector of the nuns, he meant to defend their rights, and demanded a general explanation of the episcopal intentions with regard to Sonnenburg. Thus the battle was fairly joined. The astute Abbess had managed to set the Bishop and the Duke by the ears, and her whole policy henceforth was to gain time by constantly fomenting the quarrel, and confusing the issues.

The convent was visited, at the Bishop's request, by the Prior of the famous Benedictine Abbey of Tegernsee and the Vicar-General. They found the Abbess and the nuns alike absolutely ignorant of the rule of their Order, and possessed by a most rebellious spirit. The Abbess was persuaded, by a relative, to promise resignation, on the consideration of a substantial pension. It looked as if the end of the trouble were in sight.

But there were divided counsels, and a little later we find that the insurgent Abbess had resumed control of the convent, supported by most of the nuns, who were enamoured of the lax discipline and luxurious life of the place, and were far from willing to accept the decree of Salzburg. Nicholas threatened the Abbess with excommunication and an interdict, and sent his men-at-arms for Afra von Velseck, the Prioress of the convent, who had remained faithful to him, and who had been in charge of the nuns in the interval between the resignation of the Abbess and her resumption of office. This strong action frightened the sisters, who declared themselves ready to accept reform, but on condition that the visitors of the convent should be three Abbots of their own Order, or that their submission should be to the decisions of the next synod of Salzburg. When Nicholas demanded their written submission by the 1st of August, they appealed to the Pope.

By a Bull of the 19th of October 1454, the Pope rejected the appeal of the Abbess, and directed Nicholas to depose her if she refused to submit. The priest of St. Laurent, in whose parish the convent was situated, summoned the nuns, in the name of the Bishop, to reform themselves within a month. They responded by a new appeal to Rome, and by invoking the aid of the Duke once more. A convention had been signed at Innsbrück, on the 30th of December, by which it was decided that the nuns should submit to the decision of the Benedictine Abbots of the neighbourhood.

These met at Sonnenburg in February 1455. They found that the nuns were unfaithful to their rule in many ways, for they did not regularly recite the office, they left the convent to bathe and to attend weddings, and they distributed the moneys of the foundation among themselves. The visiting Abbots having drawn up their requisitions, the nuns formally promised to obey, but forthwith represented to Sigismund that the visitors had exceeded their powers, and asked for delay. The Duke advised them to demand a translation of the statutes, and that some nuns from Salzburg or Chiemsee should be sent among them to teach them their duties! Nicholas summoned them to sign the ordinances and to conform to them by Easter. Despite the Duke's threats, Nicholas went on his way. The sentence of excommunication against the Abbess was formally drawn up at the end of April. On the 14th of June Nicholas wrote a last letter of appeal, reminding the nuns that three months had elapsed since the visit of the Abbots, and that their regulations were still disregarded. On the 20th of June the Abbess was excommunicated and deposed, the sentence being read in the churches and affixed to the gates of the convent.

Sigismund was uneasy, and attempted to revive the scheme for the retirement of the Abbess on a pension, only to be met by obstinacy on her part. At the Synod of November Nicholas solemnly renewed the excommunication. Subsequently, every Sunday, the priest of St. Laurent read the sentence of excommunication in his church before a crucifix surrounded by lighted candles, while the bells were tolled. Then, followed by the congregation, he proceeded to the door of the church, which was visible from Sonnenburg, where the lighted candles were hurled in the direction of the convent, as a symbol of damnation.[1] Nicholas had appointed Afra von Velseck to administer the convent, but the troubles did not cease. The insurgent nuns engaged a band of mercenaries, under the command of Josse Hornstein, and proceeded to enforce their claims upon the inhabitants of the three disputed valleys. The peasants organized a strong resistance, defeating the mercenaries with heavy loss, killing most of them, and capturing their commander. The contemporary accounts differ as to the numbers engaged, but it seems probable that Hornstein had some-

[1] Jaeger, *Der Streit*, i, p. 158.

where between fifty and eighty men, and that the peasants were much more numerous. Gabriel Prack, of Thurn, an officer of the Bishop's and the leader of the peasants, marched on Sonnenburg, expelled the rebellious nuns and pursued them until they found refuge in the castle of Schöneck, and restored the effective administration of the convent to Afra von Velseck.[1]

When Sigismund heard of this, he was furious. He gave orders that the nuns who were obedient to the Bishop should be expelled from the convent, and that those driven out by the peasants should be brought back again, and left there under a strong guard. Shortly afterward, however, through the mediation of the Bishop of Trent, another agreement was signed at Lüsen, by which Sigismund agreed personally to secure the resignation of the Abbess, and to select from some Benedictine convent an Abbess who could be trusted to observe the rule ; and the Bishop agreed, when the resignation was effected, and the rebellious nuns presented themselves before him, to withdraw the sentence of excommunication. For a fortnight Nicholas waited at Bruneck, vainly ; on the 14th of September 1458, he left for Rome.

However, the weary affair of Sonnenburg was really approaching its end. The Duke and the Bishop of Trent at last secured the resignation of the Abbess, and she wrote to Nicholas soliciting absolution, in the humblest terms. On the 17th of April 1459 the Vicar-General of the diocese (in the continued absence of Nicholas at Rome) confirmed the nomination of Barbara Schoendorfer as

[1] Vansteenberghe, *Nicolas de Cues*, p. 151.

Abbess of Sonnenburg, who swore obedience to
the Bishops of Brixen, and the rule of the Order,
without prejudice to 'the rights of the convent,
or those of the Duke and his successors '—a saving
clause which might easily have contained the germ
of a later dispute. The Duke recalled his men-at-
arms, who were on guard at the convent, and
Verena Stuben, that wily and stubborn nun, departed
from Sonnenburg.

The year 1453 was the most peaceful that Nicholas was to enjoy in his episcopate. It was the
period in which he wrote the *De visione Dei*, and
maintained his correspondence with the Benedictine mystics of Tegernsee. But the peace was not
to last long. Ulric von Freundsberg was cited
to appear and explain his refusal to restore to the
Bishopric the domains of Steinach and Matrei,
given in pledge fifty years before. These places
were near Innsbrück, and Sigismund took fright at
once. Nicholas answered the Duke's protests by
sending him the documents which proved the
episcopal claim, and refused to accept arbitration.
The situation changed from month to month, but
it was always full of anxiety for the Bishop. Then
in 1455 a couple of interviews between the Duke
and Nicholas at Innsbrück and at Botzen resulted
in perhaps a better accord between the two than
had ever existed. Sigismund aided the Bishop in
recovering the alienated domain of Velturns, and
Nicholas lent the Duke, who appears to have been
in chronic need of money, the sum of 3,000 florins.
At this time Sigismund declared that the Bishop
and he were ' one for life '.

But a new contest speedily arose, perhaps even

more damaging than the affair of Sonnenburg, and certainly much less creditable to Nicholas. On the death of the Bishop of Chur—a neighbouring diocese to Brixen—in 1440, the Chapter had elected Conrad von Reichberg, but, apparently at his request, Pope Eugenius IV had given the administration of the diocese to the Bishop of Constance. At the death of Conrad a dozen years later, Sigismund had secured the election of Leonard Wiesmayer (who, it will be remembered, was elected by the Chapter of Brixen, when Nicholas was appointed to the bishopric). A long struggle ensued between Wiesmayer and the Bishop of Constance. Now Wiesmayer was a Prebendary of Brixen, and Nicholas had secured from the Pope, on behalf of his nephew, Simon Wehlen, the promise of the first vacant prebend. When Wiesmayer was recognized as Bishop of Chur by the Emperor (though he was not yet recognized by Rome) Nicholas hastened to secure Wiesmayer's prebend for his nephew. On the 10th of May 1456, however, the new Pope Calixtus III quashed the election, cancelled the Bishop of Constance's authority to administer the bishopric, and conferred it upon a papal official, Antoine de Tosabetis. Hereupon Wiesmayer naturally reclaimed his prebend. Then Nicholas did the most indefensible act of his life. He remitted the decision to the Chapter of Brixen, *but charged them, under penalty of excommunication*, to confirm his nephew in the prebend, the revenues being divided between Wehlen and Wiesmayer until a final decision was reached as to the bishopric of Chur. Then if Wiesmayer did not obtain the bishopric, his prebend was to be restored to him.

The Chapter yielded to the threat, but appealed to Rome. The issue was that Wehlen kept the prebend, for Antoine de Tosabetis died within six months, and on the 12th of November 1456, Wiesmayer was confirmed in the possession of the bishopric.[1]

When the Chapter yielded to the most unjustifiable threat of the Bishop, four of the canons refused to associate themselves with this submission. Nicholas excommunicated them. Next Sunday, during Mass, they affixed a protest, in German, to the doors of the Cathedral.

Various negotiations with Sigismund ensued, and finally Nicholas promised the Duke's chancellor that he would meet Sigismund at Innsbrück on the 25th of June 1457, if those who were accusing him would also present themselves there. He began the journey on the 22nd. The same evening one of the Duke's councillors, Martin von Neideck, joined Nicholas's party at Sterzing. On leaving that place a woman conveyed a mysterious message to the Bishop to the effect that the Duke was at Matrei, with some men-at-arms, all disguised.[2] However, he arrived at Wilten without further incident. He spent the night at the Premonstratensian Abbey, and sent one of his servants on to Innsbrück to request an audience on the morrow. The Duke sent an answer to the effect that he always dedicated that day to the memory of his father, but he meant to come himself to Wilten on the day following. He seems to have set out, accompanied by two hundred

---

[1] Vansteenberghe, *Nicolas de Cues*, p. 175.
[2] Jaeger, *Der Streit*, i, p. 212.

men-at-arms, but a fall, in which he suffered some injury, served to make him return, and disperse the troop. The next morning, Nicholas rode into Innsbrück, and was received in the council chamber of the castle, where Percival von Annenberg, in the presence of the councillors of the Duke, reproached him with a long list of offences against Sigismund. Nicholas declared that he had come to take counsel with the Duke at his own request, and forthwith returned to Wilten, where he learned the same night that the Duke had occupied all the neighbouring roads with his troops. His men-at-arms were seen mounting guard around the monastery during the night.

The Cardinal had fixed his departure for the 27th. The Duke asked him to wait a day longer, and on the morrow he came to Wilten, accompanied by his councillors, and escorted by a troop of men-at-arms. An interview followed, at which the Duke's councillors tried to persuade Nicholas to prolong his stay at Wilten, or at least to give his answer to Sigismund before he went. Nicholas alleged his engagement to preach at Brixen on St. Peter's Day. The Duke cut short the conversation with a curt command. Nicholas agreed to remain, on the condition that he was to be allowed to preach.

Two days afterward, Nicholas asked for a safe-conduct, and this was brought to him the next day by three gentlemen of the Duke's household. Nicholas made known his apprehensions to these visitors; he told them that he had heard that all the roads were guarded, and that he was looked upon by everybody as a prisoner. He expressed his amazement at such treatment, and asked them

to make representations to the Duke on his behalf.
On the 2nd of July he took the road to Brixen.
He was received with demonstrations of joy, but
he had repeated warnings of the roads being occupied, at various points, by the Duke's troops, and
apparently began to fear that there would be an
attack on his episcopal residence, so the next day
he left Brixen, and by the 10th he was ensconced
in the castle of Andraz, at the southern limit of his
diocese, and the point where he was nearest the
territory of Venice. He wrote to the Doge for
permission to recruit a bodyguard of Venetian
mercenaries, and at the same time acquainted the
Pope with his situation.[1]

The letter caused considerable alarm and anger
in Rome. The Pope wrote to Ludwig of Bavaria,
and the Bishop of Chur, asking them to send help
to Nicholas, and he sent a message to Sigismund,
demanding that he should give the Cardinal his
liberty within eight days, and cease his policy of
enmity, under penalty of an interdict. Sigismund
had anticipated the Pope's threat, and, advised
by his jurists, had previously published a protest
and an appeal to the Pope better informed. Two
members of the Duke's entourage carried copies of
these documents to Nicholas at Andraz, along with
a passport sealed by Sigismund, the Bishop of
Chur, and the Counts of Lüpfen and Kirchberg.
The Cardinal declared that he did not need the
passport, since he already had the Duke's written
promise of protection for his whole life. In fact,
Nicholas seems at this juncture to have adopted a
particularly irreconcilable attitude. He was receiv-

[1] Vansteenberghe, *Nicolas de Cues*, p. 181.

ing constant warnings of attempts against his person intended by the Duke. Much of this information came indirectly from members of the Duke's household, and it is difficult to believe that it was all unfounded rumour. Nicholas believed it, in any case, and he wrote a letter to the Duke with the extravagant demand that Sigismund should cede to the Bishops of Brixen, as the only way of securing their liberty and independence, the castles of Roedeneck, Gufidaun and Welturn, which, by their proximity to Brixen, were a constant menace. Various negotiations followed between Nicholas, and his Chapter, and the representatives of the Duke. The Chapter had been for some time past counselling Nicholas to compromise. They warned him that the threat of the interdict was irritating the faithful, that a popular rising was feared, and that military preparations were being made. Nicholas told them roundly that they feared the Duke more than they feared God. Finally Nicholas promised to suspend the interdict until the return of the Duke, who was absent for some length of time. He met Sigismund at Lüsen in August, and the meeting was amicable; indeed, through the efforts of the Duchess and the Bishop of Trent, it promised a reconciliation. A further meeting was arranged for the 23rd of April 1459, by which time Nicholas expected to be back from Rome. The Cardinal returned to Bruneck, and preached there on the 8th of September 1458—the last sermon, as it proved, that he ever did preach in his diocese. A few days later he left for Italy, and entered Rome on the last day of September.[1]

[1] Vansteenberghe, *Nicolas de Cues*, p. 187.

Several weeks earlier, Aeneas Sylvius, an old friend of Nicholas, had ascended the papal chair as Pius II. The new Pope, months before his elevation, had urged Nicholas to return to Rome: 'Such abilities as yours should not be suffered to languish', he wrote, 'imprisoned among snows and gloomy defiles.'[1] Accordingly Nicholas was well received, and the Pope on his departure for the congress of Princes at Mantua,[2] a few months afterward, named Nicholas his Vicar-General in temporal affairs, that is to say, Governor of Rome and of the papal territories. In this office Nicholas seems to have proved extremely successful. He put down the disorders that were prevalent in the city and the Campagna, held in check the contentious nobles of the city, organized a gendarmerie and, with an eye on the financial needs of the coming Crusade, succeeded in increasing the produce of the salt works. Though his commission related only to temporalities, his authority as Legate enabled him to visit the greater basilicas, to assist in the reform of the monasteries of Italy, and to hold a synod in the pontifical Chapel.

[1] Aeneas Sylvius, *Opera* (Basel, 1571), p. 765. The letter is dated Rome, 28 Dec. 1457.
[2] On the 11th of January 1459. The Bishop of Ferrara was Vicar-General in spiritual affairs.

CHAPTER IV

LAST DAYS AND DEATH

THE Pope was on terms of friendship with Sigismund, as well as with Nicholas, and he was hoping to effect a reconciliation between them when he met the Duke at Mantua. In spite of repeated invitations Sigismund did not appear there until the 10th of November 1459. The Duke's cause against Nicholas was managed by a skilled jurist in his service, Gregory Heimburg. He was rather a remarkable man. Born in Franconia, he had studied law at Padua, where he had been a contemporary, or almost a contemporary, of Nicholas. He had attended the Council of Basel, as representing the Archbishop of Mainz, and had more or less opposed Nicholas there, in the affair of Ulric von Manderscheid. Afterward, he had been in the service of the city of Nuremberg, of King Ladislas of Bohemia, and of the Archduke Albert of Austria, whence in May 1458, he passed into that of Sigismund.[1] He had consistently taken the side of the Council and of the Empire against the Pope, and he exhibited a good deal of

[1] Gregory von Heimburg was probably a native of Würzburg. He died at Dresden in August 1472, and is buried in the Barfüsserkirche there. See, for his career, C. Brockhaus, *Gregor von Heimburg*, and particularly pp. 149–220 for the strife at Brixen.

personal animosity against Nicholas. The accession of Gregory Heimburg to the ranks of the Duke's counsellors seems to have reacted promptly upon Sigismund's behaviour. Hardly was Nicholas out of the diocese when the Duke seized upon the fact that Nicholas had secured sworn statements from some peasants as to what had recently happened, to declare a breach of the truce, and to assemble a Diet at Sterzing where all his grievances against the Cardinal were ventilated.

It was not until the 10th of November 1459 that Sigismund presented himself at Mantua. He was received with much pomp, and accorded an audience with the Pope.[1]   Later the cause between the Duke and the Cardinal was formally argued before the Pope. Gregory Heimburg presented the case, and charged Nicholas with misusing his ecclesiastical powers, and with assailing the honour of the Duke by accusing Sigismund of designs upon his life. The Cardinal, on his part, set forth the ancient rights of the Bishops of Brixen, and contended that Sigismund, as Count of the Tyrol, was his vassal. The Pope tried to mediate, but Heimburg refused in advance all offers of arbitration, and took his stand upon the Salzburg agreement which Nicholas had signed eight years before. He also contended that all temporal matters at issue were beyond the authority of the Pope, and pertained to the Emperor. On the 29th of November 1459, the Duke left Mantua (with several ecclesiastical favours from the Pope as a parting gift), but his legal representatives remained behind.

[1] Jaeger, *Der Streit*, i, p. 331.

Various efforts at mediation by the Pope and the Markgraf of Baden proved fruitless.

Nicholas had already made up his mind to return to his diocese. The Pope agreed, but asked the Duke for an assurance that he would not sanction any act hostile to the Cardinal. On the 14th of February the Duke's troops, who were occupying the Pustherthal, ostensibly because of the menace of war with Carinthia, suddenly took possession of the convent of Sonnenburg. Nicholas, who was at Bruneck when he heard the news, fled to the castle of Andraz. His apprehensions were increased by an attack made upon one of his vehicles by the Duke's men-at-arms, at Mühlbach, when he was on the way to the Synod. He expressed his indignation before the assembly, and proceeded to proclaim the interdict according to the Bull of Calixtus III, binding the ecclesiastics to observe it under penalty of suspension, and threatening that, if an accord were not reached before Easter, he would not consecrate the holy oils. To these announcements he added the extraordinary threat that if there were any further check to the negotiations between himself and the Duke, he would give all the fiefs of the bishopric to the Emperor. The retort of Sigismund was immediate. He convoked the nobility of the neighbourhood at Innsbrück, gathered troops, and on the 12th of April declared war on the Cardinal and marched against him at the head of an army of 500 horsemen and 3,000 infantry.[1]

Nicholas heard of this on the morning of Easter Day, while he was preparing to celebrate Mass and

[1] Vansteenberghe, *Nicolas de Cues*, p. 196.

preach. His first instinct was to fly, but he was too late. He threw himself, with five companions, into the castle, which overlooks the town of Bruneck. The Chapter sent to the Duke requesting him to desist from an attack on the person of the Cardinal, and Nicholas himself offered to remit the matters alleged against him in the declaration of war to the decision of three of the Duke's own counsellors, but both messages were in vain. After a demonstration by the Duke's troops, the town gates were opened, and presently the castle was surrounded. Nicholas protested in vain. On Tuesday the Duke invested the castle and opened fire.[1]

There was nothing to do but surrender. Hostilities ceased at noon on Wednesday, and the castle was given up to the Duke. After negotiations, lasting a couple of hours, Nicholas agreed to yield up to the Duke the domain of Taufers (recently purchased from him); to remit a debt of 3,000 florins; to give the castles belonging to the bishopric into the charge of the Chapter, who were to appoint as custodians persons acceptable to the Duke; to remit the dispute about the mines of Gastein to the arbitration of the Archduke Albert of Austria; to request from the Pope the raising of the interdict and the absolution of the Duke; and finally to pay a ransom of 10,000 florins.[2] Against this enormous submission there was nothing to set on the part of Sigismund but a few conventional expressions—he pledged himself once

[1] On the attack upon Bruneck, see Scharpff, *Reformator*, p. 306 ff., and Jaeger, *Der Streit*, ii, pp. 11–14.
[2] Ibid., ii, p. 15.

more to protect the Chapter and the household of the Bishop; and he expressed regret for his misdemeanours, and a desire for absolution.

The Cardinal left Bruneck on the 27th of April. Three days before the Duke had insisted on his giving a formal confirmation in writing of his promises. Nicholas appears to have done so quite readily; he had already made up his mind to repudiate this, and all his other engagements, on the ground that they were extorted from him by force while he was a prisoner. Accordingly, as soon as he was free, he suspended the priest who had celebrated Mass at Bruneck in the presence of the Duke, and laid an interdict on the town. On his journey into Italy he wrote from Ampezzo protesting the nullity of his recent acts. Upon the arrival of Nicholas at Rome, Sigismund was summoned to appear before the consistory at Siena. He sent one of his jurists, Blumenau, with an appeal to the Pope better informed. Blumenau was thrown into prison, as suspected of heresy, but escaped, and succeeded in reaching the Tyrol. The Pope took the diocese of Brixen under his own administration, and launched against the Duke and his partisans the greater excommunication.

Events now moved rapidly to a climax. The Pope could not possibly pass by the treatment that Sigismund had meted out to the Cardinal, a prelate in the Pope's own language, 'whose merit and whose goodness were known to the whole of Christendom'.[1] The Emperor Frederick III also declared to the Papal Nuncio that he condemned

[1] Letter to Sigismund dated 27th April 1460, in the Archive of the Vatican.

the action of Sigismund, not only because he loved and venerated Nicholas for his virtues, but because, in any case, he held justice and the rights of the Church in higher regard than his relationship to Sigismund. The latter addressed a manifesto to Christendom (especially to all Christian princes, whose rights, he maintained, were involved in the dispute), in which he appealed from Pius to a future Pope or a future Council.

The dominions of Sigismund were placed under an interdict, and the diocese of Brixen was taken under the protection of the Pope until the return of the Bishop. The Pope wrote to the cities of Trent, Basel, Kempten, Constance and Nuremberg, to the Doge of Venice, and the German merchants in that city, and to the Bishops of Augsburg, Freising, and Constance, demanding their aid in the enforcement of the interdict, and in the isolation of the Tyrol. The Emperor promised military aid, and the Swiss, who had been practically held back by the Pope for six months past, were eager to invade the Ducal territories. On the other hand, the nearest neighbours of the Duke were not eager to offend him. The Archbishop of Salzburg had not fulfilled the Pope's command to administer the diocese of Brixen three months after the command had been given ; the Bishop of Trent did not publish the interdict ; [1] and the town of Kempten disregarded the Pope's letter. Sigismund endeavoured to influence the Emperor to suggest the dismissal of Nicholas, and the appointment of another Bishop in his place ; he tried also, through his relative James II of Scotland, to induce the King

[1] Duex, *Nicolaus von Cusa*, ii, p. 203.

6

of France to hold back the Swiss ; and he renewed
his alliance with the Swabian nobles.   However,
the Swiss cantons declared war, and a good deal of
the Tyrol was speedily overrun by their troops.
Sigismund had to sue for peace, and negotiations
began at Constance in the middle of October.
The Pope tried to dissuade the Swiss from making
peace, but they knew that the conflict might easily
enlarge itself, and leave them in a much less
favourable position.   The King of Bohemia gave
them a serious warning, and they were aware that
an alliance against them was contemplated between
the Markgraf of Baden and Count Ulric of Wür-
temberg.   Peace was signed on the 7th of December
1460.   The Duke lost the whole of Thurgovia, but
the blockade of his territory was broken through.[1]

The Pope was indignant both at the action of the
Swiss in concluding peace and at the disregard of
his mandates by some of the Bishops.   He sent a
letter to the German princes, on the last day of
1460, and followed it, in the next month, by a Bull
in which Gregory Heimburg, the Bishop of Trent,
the Abbess of Sonnenburg, and several others, are
summoned to appear and answer for their conduct.
This was published throughout Switzerland and
Southern Germany, and the results appeared
speedily.   The Archbishop of Salzburg sent for
Simon Wehlen, confided to him the administration
of the diocese of Brixen, and published the interdict.   The Bishop of Trent also changed his
attitude, and sent messengers to Rome to answer
the charges against him.   The Bishop of Augsburg
refused absolution to those who traded with the

[1] Vansteenberghe, *Nicolas de Cues*, p. 202.

valley of the Adige or frequented the marches of
Botzen and Meran. Meanwhile Gregory Heimburg
had issued a violent pamphlet appealing to all
who loved justice, and all who sympathized with the
oppressed. It found its way to Rome, and on the
16th of March it was affixed to the walls in all the
four quarters of the city, but the people tore it
down.[1] The pamphlet was not without effect
outside of Italy. The King of Bohemia and the
Archduke Albrecht entered afresh into an understanding with Sigismund. The Chapter of Brixen
appointed Wolfgang Neidlinger administrator of
the diocese, despite the express prohibition of the
Pope, and, in the name of the canons who had been
cited to appear, appealed to the Pope better
informed.[2] At a consistory held on the 1st of
April 1461, Gregory Heimburg was declared guilty
of heresy, but sixty days' grace was accorded the
persons who had been summoned to appear.
Several things counselled the Pope to prudent
action. The Elector of Mainz, an excommunicate
person, had appealed to a future general Council,
and had gained important support within the
Empire. Ludwig of Bavaria had concluded an
alliance with Sigismund. The Diet of Mainz, in
May, received the delegates of the Duke and of the
Chapter of Brixen, but the Papal Legate (who was
Rudolph von Rudesheim, the Dean of Münster) succeeded in averting any decision adverse to the Pope.

After this, the weary dispute narrowed its scope,
and the danger of the Pope's conduct of the affair
leading to a general revolt against the Holy See

[1] Pastor, *Geschichte der Päpste*, ii, p. 134.
[2] Vansteenberghe, *Nicolas de Cues*, pp. 203-4.

passed by, but the controversy dragged on for a year or two. In these last years it has less concern for the biography of Nicholas; it was still, of course, essentially a dispute as to his conduct and administration, but he had much less personal connexion with it. The Papacy had become the principal party on the one side, and not the Bishop. There were letters and pamphlets by Gregory Heimburg, and replies from Theodore Lelio, the Bishop of Feltre, in defence of Nicholas; there were various reprisals by Sigismund upon the clergy and the religious who were loyal to Nicholas and Rome; there were long negotiations in which the French Court, the Duke of Milan, the Duke of Bavaria, the Swiss cantons, the Republic of Venice, the Archbishop of Augsburg, the Archbishop of Salzburg, and the Bishop of Constance and others, were all involved; there was another attempt at a blockade of the Tyrol, and there was a preaching crusade against the Duke by Franciscan friars.

The Doge of Venice, appealed to as an arbitrator, had appointed Paul Morosini to act, and he seems to have brought the dispute almost to a settlement on the basis of an indemnity of 28,000 gulden to be paid by the Duke, but this Nicholas refused to accept. Then the Emperor Frederick III interposed, and this brought about the final settlement. The death of the Archduke of Styria put an end to the war in which the Emperor had been engaged on one side, and Sigismund on the other. Thus reconciled with his cousin, the Emperor attempted to reconcile him and the Cardinal. Conferences were held at Vienna beginning early in the year 1464. The settlement was reached on the 25th of

August 1464. It was a compromise, like most such settlements. Nicholas was to be reinstated with all the episcopal rights and powers intact; Sigismund was to restore the domain of Taufers and all else that he had seized after the assault on Bruneck; the Bishop was to invest the Duke with all the fiefs which provided the episcopal revenues. Thus there were mutual concessions, but on the whole it was a victory for the Church, and a humiliation for Sigismund, who had to sue, through the Emperor, for pardon and absolution from the Papal Legate. On the 2nd of September the excommunication and the interdict were revoked. Nicholas died three weeks before.

He had been seriously ill at Rome in June and July 1461, *gravissima infirmitate valde debilitatus*, as he wrote, a month or two afterward, to the Bishop of Padua. He was restored to health in the favourable climate of Orvieto, where he went on the advice of Peter Barbo. He spent most of the summer of 1462 and of 1463 in the same place. His last days were occupied with the affair of Bohemia. The Pope had been pressing for the embassy which Podiebrad had promised, before his coronation, that he would send to Rome to declare the obedience of Bohemia. This arrived in March 1462. The envoys offered the obedience of the King of Bohemia, but took their stand upon the *Compactata*—the concordat which had been settled with the Council of Basel. The matter was referred to a Committee of Cardinals, of whom Nicholas of Cusa, Carvajal, and Bessarion were the most prominent. The answer was given to the envoys in a public consistory on the 31st of March.

The Pope annulled the Compacts. Thus Nicholas assisted (for he was present and approved) at the destruction of the very agreement which, nearly thirty years before, he had had a large share in making. The next day the Bohemian envoys left Rome. They had asked that some one should accompany them to represent to the King the Pope's position and demands. The Pope commissioned for this purpose Fantin de Valle, a Dalmatian priest, who had been acting as Podiebrad's proctor at Rome. After an interview with Fantin, the King referred the matter to a Diet held at Prague in August 1462. The result was a definite breach with Rome.

The Pope, after some negotiations with the representative of Breslau, in which Nicholas of Cusa took a prominent part, cancelled the convention by which the city had given allegiance to the King. But Podiebrad had an ally in the Emperor, who requested the Pope to restore Breslau to the allegiance of the Bohemian King. The city made urgent appeals, through its representative, to Nicholas of Cusa. He and Cardinal Francis Piccolomini wrote urgently to the Pope, and the latter in April 1464 announced that he had appointed the Cardinal-Bishop of Brixen and the Cardinal-Bishop of Spoleto as judges in the question. At a consistory, held on the 16th of June 1464, the King of Bohemia was cited to appear. Next day the Pope left Rome for Ancona, where he awaited the arrival of Nicholas to reduce the citation to proper juristic forms. It was on his way thither [1] that Nicholas

[1] It has often been stated that Nicholas was on his way to Leghorn to inspect the fleet which the Genoese were equip-

was seized with his last illness, at Todi, and after
lingering in the Bishop's Palace for three weeks,
he died there on the 11th of August 1464.

When Nicholas was ill at Rome, in the summer
of 1461, he had made his will with the assistance of
Henry Pomert, his secretary.[1] It is dated the
15th of June and is witnessed by John Stam [2]
and Peter Erkelenz.[3] On the 6th of August 1464,
when he was dying, he executed the same testament
afresh,[4] probably for the sake of adding some

ping against the Turks. This is a complete mistake. It
was Cardinal Nicholas Forteguerri (a relative of the Pope's)
who was sent to Leghorn. See Scharpff, *Reformator*, p. 229 ;
Vansteenberghe, *Nicolas de Cues*, p. 227 ; Creighton, *History
of the Papacy*, iii, p. 244.

[1] Pomert, a native of Lübeck, was a notary at Brixen
when Nicholas became Bishop. He accompanied the Cardinal on his legation, and became his chaplain. At the date
of the will he had been for some years Canon of Lübeck.
Vansteenberghe, *Nicolas de Cues*, p. 457.

[2] Stam belonged to Trèves, and had become, in 1460,
Canon of St. Simeon and Prebendary of St. Paulinus there.
Two years later he was Canon of St. Florin at Coblenz,
and about the same time he was also acting as chaplain to
the Cardinal. His association with Nicholas began at least
fifteen years before the date of the will, not later than the
commencement of the Cardinal's work as Legate. Vansteenberghe, *Nicolas de Cues*, p. 457.

[3] Peter Wynmari of Erkelenz had also been Nicholas's
secretary. He held the benefice of Prutz in the diocese of
Brixen, and later in life was Dean of St. Mary at Aix-la-
Chapelle, and Chamberlain to the Pope. Vansteenberghe,
Nicolas de Cues, p. 277 ; Scharpff, *Nicolaus von Cusa*, pp.
213–14.

[4] The will is in full in Marx, *Stiftungen*, pp. 226–31, and
in Uebinger, *Zur Lebensgeschichte des Nikolaus Cusanus*, in
the *Historisches Jahrbuch des Görres-Gesellschaft*, xiv, pp. 553–
9. It states that the Cardinal had *in Banco de Medicis sex*

clauses which explain that the amounts of money mentioned in the earlier will are to be reckoned as considerably less, partly because of what has been spent since, and partly because of a different valuation of the silver.[1]   This will was executed in the presence of Paul Toscanelli, his friend of forty years past, Ferdinand Martins, his physician, John Andrew Bussi, the Bishop of Accia,[2] John

millia et septingentos florenos Rhenenses, of which five thousand are given to the Hospital at Cues.   The Medici Bank had an office in the financial quarter of Rome, in the neighbourhood of the Canal del Ponte, the street called to-day Via del Banco di Santo Spirito.   See Gregorovius, *Geschichte der Stadt Rom im Mittelalter*, vii, pp. 699–700.

[1] Scharpff, *Nicolaus von Cusa*, p. 380.

[2] Giovanni Andrea de' Bussi, a native of Vigevano, once the Cardinal's secretary.   The description of him as *episcopus Acciensi* has puzzled the earlier biographers.   For he was Bishop of Aleria for some nine years before his death in 1475, and there seemed to be no record of his holding the see of Accia, also in Corsica, at an earlier date.   The contemporary Bishops of Accia are recorded, in one standard authority, as Albert de Cassini, appointed in 1453, and Bartholomew, appointed in 1480.   See Gams, *Series Episcoporum Ecclesiae Catholicae*, pp. 765–6.   But this record is defective.   As a matter of fact, Bussi succeeded the excommunicated Bishop of Accia in 1463, and was translated to Aleria in 1466.   See Eubel, *Hierarchia Catholica Medii Aevi*, ii, pp. 78, 84.

It is interesting to notice that Bussi had a very definite contact with the new art of printing, and that Nicholas of Cusa, according to him, was deeply interested in it.   Bussi established the first printing press in Italy at the Benedictine monastery of Subiaco in 1465.   In the dedication of a volume, which appeared in Rome about 1468–70, Bussi says that his old friend and patron Nicholas *peroptobat ut haec sancta ars, quae oriri tunc videbatur in Germania Romam deduceretur.*

Römer,[1] and Peter Erkelenz, who acted as apostolic and imperial notary.[2]

The body of Nicholas was taken to Rome and buried in his titular church, San Pietro in Vincoli. There was an enormous crowd at the funeral, and widespread lamentation for his death among the populace of Rome—much more, declared a contemporary, than for the death of Pius II. There is a monument in the church, on the left of the nave, the work of Andrea Bregno, with the inscription:

> *Qui iacet ante tuas Nicolaus, Petre, catenas,*
> *Hoc opus erexit. Cetera marmor habet.*

The Cardinal is represented on his knees, his hands joined in prayer. The actual tombstone, near the monument, bears a figure of the Cardinal, the head resting upon cushions and w aring a mitre, the hands crossed upon a chasuble. The inscription beneath is: *Dilexit Deum, timuit et veneratus est, ac illi soli servivit. Promissio retributionis non fefellit eum. Vixit annis LXIII,* and around the slab: *Nicolaus de Cusa Treveren. Sancti Petri ad vincula cardinalis, Brixinen episcopus. Tuderti obiit MCCCCLXIIII, XI Augusti. Ob devocionem cathenarum sancti Petri hic sepeliri voluit.*[3]

The Cardinal devoted most of his wealth to the Hospital of St. Nicholas at Cues. He had executed a testament in 1450, fourteen years earlier, in connexion with the foundation of the Hospital. The

---

[1] Römer, a relative of the Cardinal's, on his mother's side, was Canon of St. Florin at Coblenz, and became Rector of the Hospital of St. Nicholas at Cues. Vansteenberghe, *Nicolas de Cues,* p. 5.   [2] Marx, *Stiftungen,* p. 226.
[3] Vansteenberghe, *Nicolas de Cues,* pp. 461–2.

purpose had been in his mind for some years before this, but the actual fulfilment of it began then, about the fiftieth year of his age. He obtained two Bulls in August 1450, permitting him to mortgage and manipulate in other ways the income of his numerous benefices. The actual building of the Chapel of the Hospital began before the 1st of May 1453, the date of a Bull according an indulgence to those who visited it in course of construction. It was finished by the 5th of May 1457. On the 3rd of December 1458, at Rome, Nicholas executed a deed containing detailed instructions as to the administration of the Hospital.[1] He obtained a Bull from the Pope on the 2nd of January 1459, in which the Hospital is taken under the special jurisdiction of the Holy See, and all its endowments and privileges are confirmed. The value of Nicholas's legacy is stated at 20,000 florins. The next month he obtained the privilege of a portable altar for the Chapel, pending the consecration of the building. The latter ceremony, which Nicholas had hoped to conduct himself, did not take place until 1465, the year after his death.

The building of the hospital cost 10,000 Rhenish gold florins, the equivalent of something like £10,000 in modern money.[2] Nicholas endowed it with 20,000 Rhenish gold florins, to produce a yearly revenue of 800 florins,[3] say, a capital of £20,000 producing an income of £800, in modern values. The hospital was to shelter thirty-three poor men—the number was chosen because of the

[1] Scharpff, *Nicolaus von Cusa*, pp. 387–96.
[2] Marx, *Stiftungen*, p. 170.
[3] Scharpff, *Nicolaus von Cusa*, p. 383.

radition as to the years of our Lord's life on earth
—who were to be not less than fifty years of age,
ind amongst them, if possible, six priests, and six
nobles. It was to be a place of study, as well as a
place of refuge, and the library received the Cardinal's collection of manuscripts.[1] The hospital
has escaped the drums and tramplings of more than
hree conquests, and still exists at Cues, much as
t was when it was founded. The heart of Nicholas
s buried in a leaden casket before the altar in the
Chapel.[2] The place is marked by a copper plaque

[1] The library still contains about 300 of the Cardinal's
manuscripts. These have been described by Dr. F. X.
Kraus, in some interesting articles contributed to the *Leipzig Serapeum* in 1864 and 1865, entitled *Die Handschriften-
Sammlung des Cardinals Nicolaus von Cusa*, and by Dr. J.
Marx, in *Verzeichnis der Handschriften-Sammlung des Hospitals
zu Cues* (1905). See also Rotta, *Il Cardinale Nicolò di Cusa*,
pp. 247–82. There are five Hebrew MSS., of which two
contain a part of the Old Testament (viz. the Prophetical
books, according to the arrangement of the Hebrew Bible),
and the rest are collections of Synagogue prayers and chants.
There are five Greek MSS.—the Homilies of St. Chrysostom, the Commentary of Nicetas on Gregory Nazianzen,
a Catena of the Greek Fathers on St. John's Gospel, and
two Greek and Latin parallel Psalters, one containing only
Pss. 109–50. The rest of the MSS. are Latin. Many of
the Fathers are represented—Ambrose, Anselm, Augustine,
Cyprian, Gregory the Great, Hilary, Isidore, Jerome, Leo,
Tertullian, and, in Latin translations, Athanasius, Chrysostom, Cyril, Eusebius, Origen. There is more than one
copy of the pseudo-Dionysius. Among later writers there
are Boethius, Raymond Lull, Duns Scotus, and Thomas
Aquinas. There are many of the works of Plato and Aristotle, and Proclus's *Theologia Platonis*, and his exposition of
the *Parmenides*. There are no less than fifty-eight MSS. on
the *Jus canonicum*—this is by far the largest section of the library.

[2] Marx, *Stiftungen*, p. 166.

with a portrait of the Cardinal and the inscription : *Nicolao de Cusa tit. s. Petri ad vincula presbytero Cardinali et Episcopo Brixin., qui obiit Tuderti huius hospitalis fundator, MCCCCLXIIII die XI Augusti et ob devocionem Romae ante cathenas s. Petri sepeliri voluit.*

The text quoted on the monument in Rome follows, and then : *Vixit annis LXIII, Deo et hominibus charus.* The inscription ends : *Benefactori suo munificentissimo P. de Ercklens Decanus aquensis faciendum curavit*, 1488.[1]

Nicholas founded, in addition to the Hospital at Cues, the *Bursa Cusana* for twenty clerical students. The course of study was to last for seven years, and to be pursued at the College of Deventer. A house was built there for the scholars' residence, after the Cardinal's death, by Theodore von Xanten, who was the Rector of the Hospital of St. Nicholas. This institution was endowed with a capital of 5,000 Rhenish gold florins.[2] It came to an end during the seventeenth century.[3]

[1] Vansteenberghe, *Nicolas de Cues*, p. 462.

[2] Scharpff, *Nicolaus von Cusa*, p. 383.

[3] The house stood in the street which is still named the Bursensteeg ; there is an infant school on the site to-day. The institution underwent many vicissitudes from the time of the Reformation onward, and in 1682 the Magistrates of Deventer decided upon a policy of sequestration, and in place of maintenance, gave the students a yearly pension of a certain amount. The authorities of the Hospital of St. Nicholas at Cues have made several attempts to recover the revenues by process of law, but always unsuccessfully. I owe these particulars to an interesting pamphlet by a Dutch antiquary, *De Bursa Cusana te Deventer*, van Dr. J. Muller, which was lent me by the great kindness of Dr. J. C. van Slee, of Diepenveen.

II

THE WRITINGS OF NICHOLAS OF CUSA

THERE are four more or less complete editions of Nicholas's writings. The first was printed not later than 1490,[1] probably by Martin Flach, of Strasburg. It is a small black letter folio in two volumes, or rather in two parts. The parts are not numbered, and there is no pagination, so that when the two parts are bound together, as they generally are, they are not always in the same order. The British Museum possesses two copies of the whole work (in which what is probably the proper order of the two parts is reversed),[2] and one copy of what the catalogue describes as the second part, and probably ought to describe as the first. This early and rare edition is a very interesting production. There are no printed initials either in the titles of the various works, or at the beginning of the chapters ; in the British Museum copies these have been written in and illuminated. Each part is prefaced with the same prologue, which

[1] There is a copy in the Stadtbibliothek at Trèves which was originally presented to the Hospital of St. Nicholas at Cues by Peter Erkelenz, the Cardinal's secretary and friend, in 1490. The date of this gift furnishes the *terminus ad quem* for determining the date of the edition.

[2] Catalogued as I. B. 2267–8 (formerly 3705 e. e. 5) and I. B. 2265–6 (formerly 3705 e. e. 6).

begins: *Prohemium*: *In hoc volumine continentur certi tractatus et libri altissime contemplacionis et doctrine: a preclare memorie prestantissimo doctissimoque viro Nico. de Cusa Sacros° Ro. eccl° tit¹ Si Petri ad v. presbytero cardinali* . . . and ends with a list of the works contained in that part. The lists are as follows:

Part 1. *De docta ignorantia. Apologia docte ignorantie. De coniecturis. De filiatione dei. Dyalogus de Genesi. Ydiote.*

Part 2. *De visione dei. De pace fidei. Reparatio kalendarij. De mathematicis complementis. Cribratio alchoran. De venatione sapientiae. De ludo globi. Compendium. Trialogus de possest. Contra bohemos. De mathematica perfectione. De berillo. De dato patris luminum. De querendo deum. Dyalogus de apice theorie.*[1]

The second edition of Nicholas's works was printed by Stefano Dolcino, at Milan, about 1505, in two quarto volumes.[2] It is a slavish reprint of the first edition, but in Roman type. It has the same prologue, the various works are printed in the same order, and there are the same arbitrary variations in spelling. In some copies the *De ludo globi* and the *Compendium* are missing; in other copies the *De mathematica perfectione* and the *De beryllo*; and in others the epistle dedicatory. This

[1] The above description is from a personal examination of the book in the British Museum. A copy in the University Library at Halle has been described by Dr. A. Richter in the *Zeitschrift für Philosophie*, lxxviii, pp. 285–6.

Dr. Richter gives a list of the contents of the two parts which agrees with that I have given in the text.

[2] In the British Museum exemplar the two volumes or parts are bound in one.

last, which is the distinguishing feature of the edition, is a letter written by Roland, the Marquis Pallavicini (who bore the cost of printing the edition), to the apostolic legate, Georges d'Amboise, Cardinal Archbishop of Rouen, who was in Milan in 1500, representing Louis XII of France. The letter is dated 1502, and we learn from it that Pallavicini had been introduced to the writings of Nicholas by Jerome Tornielli, the Vicar-General of the Observants.

The third edition, in three volumes, was issued at Paris in 1514 by Jacques Lefèvre of Étaples (*Jacobus Faber Stapulensis*), the famous humanist. He was a convinced Reformer, though he never broke with Rome, always hoping for reform from within. He had a variegated career, and was at one time tutor to the children of Francis I, and librarian of the royal castle of Blois. He owed his life, when things grew menacing for the adherents of the Reformation in France, to the protection of the Queen of Navarre, who gave him asylum at her residence at Nérac, where he spent the rest of his life, dying in 1536. His interest in Nicholas of Cusa was probably due to the Cardinal's activity in regard to the reform of the Church. Lefèvre prefaced to the edition a letter addressed to Dionysius de Briçonnet, who was then Bishop of Toulon, and later, Bishop of Lodève (St. Malo).

Lefèvre was active in seeking copies of works by Nicholas which were not contained in the earlier editions, and applied to learned acquaintances all over Europe. He succeeded in making some important additions, notably the *Concordantia catholica*, and the *Exercitationum*, in ten books—the material of the latter being got from the volumes of the Cardinal's sermons preserved at Rome.

The mention of another sixteenth-century edition, supposed to be printed at Nuremberg, appears to be a pure mistake on the part of a bibliographer.[1] It probably arose from the fact that there was printed at Nuremberg in 1533 or 1534 a volume which contained, along with the works of Regiomontanus, the famous German astronomer, some of Nicholas's smaller mathematical works.

The fourth edition of the complete works of Nicholas, and the last, appeared at Basel, in 1565, in three volumes, edited by Heinrich Petri. He was the third in succession of a famous family of printers. He was knighted by the Emperor Charles V in 1556, and he and his successors thereafter used the name Henric-Petri, in distinction from others who bore the name of Petri. He died in 1579. This edition added to the contents of the Paris edition some mathematical tracts (especially the *De quadratura circuli*), which had appeared some thirty years before, among the writings of Regiomontanus. This Basel edition is in every respect the best.

It should be remarked that the last tract which appears in this edition, *Correctio tabularum Alphonsii* (i.e. an emendation of the astronomical tables prepared by King Alphonso the Tenth of Castile, in the thirteenth century), is not the work of Nicholas. It consists, as Duhem has shown, of three fragments.[2] The first and largest is from a tract,

[1] Fabricius, *Bibliotheca latina mediae et infimae aetatis*, i, p. 405.

[2] Duhem, *Le Système du Monde*, iv, pp. 21-2.

probably by Geoffrey of Meaux, entitled *Expositio tabularum Alfonsi et motiva probantia falsitatem earum*, dated 1347 in one manuscript, and annotated by the fifteenth-century transcriber : *Credo per Gaufredum de Meldis*. This is followed by two other fragments from William of St. Cloud and Henry Bate of Malines. It is evident that Nicholas had these pieces copied for him, because of their bearing upon the reform of the Calendar, and that after his death they were taken for his own composition.

All the editions appear to be ultimately based upon the autograph manuscripts of Nicholas, some of which are still preserved in the Hospital at Cues.[1]

The early writings of Nicholas in connexion with the Council of Basel have been dealt with already, in the account of his life—the *De concordantia catholica*, the *De auctoritate praesidendi in concilio generale*, the *De reparatione Calendarii*, and the *Epistolae ad Bohemos*. The earliest of his philosophical works is the *De docta ignorantia*, and it is

---

[1] Weitaus die wichtigsten Handschriften sind E2 und E3 in der Bibliothek des St. Nicholas Hospitals zu Cues. Auf diesen nämlich, dem kalligraphisch geschriebenen Handexemplar des Autors, beruhen in erster Linie die Gesammtausgaben : 1. die Inkunabel s. l. a. typ., erschienen (nach Holtrop, *Catalogus libr. saec. XV. impressorum* Nr. 687) um 1448 zu Strassburg bei Martin Flach ; 2. die Pariser 1514 ; und 3. die Basler Ausgabe 1565. Fabricius nennt ausserdem auch noch eine Nürnberger Ausgabe 1514, hat dieselbe aber augenscheinlich niemals gesehen. Anlass zu dieser schwerlich richtigen Angabe bot höchstwahrscheinlich jener Druck, welcher zu Nürnberg 1534 erschien und einiges von Cusanus, was sich ungedruckt in Nachlasse des Regiomontanus befand, der Öffentlichkeit übergab. Uebinger, *Die philosophischen Schriften des Nikolaus Cusanus*, in *Zeitschrift für Philosophie*, 103, p. 66.

first in importance as well as in date. It contains the whole of his system, and that system was never really modified, except in respect of some formulae which he seems to have tried, all his life long, to make more subtle and more exact, and which will be dealt with in due course. He began the work on the 19th of December 1439, in the cloister of Münstermaifeld, where he was Provost.[1] He finished it on the 12th of February 1440 in his home at Cues.[2]

His next work was the *De coniecturis*, which probably dates from the same year. It cannot in any case be later than 1444,[3] since it was in that year that Cardinal Cesarini, Nicholas's old friend and patron, died ; both books are dedicated to him. The *De coniecturis* is second in interest and importance, as it is in date, to the *De docta ignorantia*. The very close connexion between the thought of the two works is a strong presumption that the *De coniecturis* dates from 1440.

The *De quaerendo Deum* was written at Mainz,[4] in 1445, and the *De dato Patris luminum*[5] either late in that, or early in the following year. The

[1] Scharpff, *Nicolaus von Cusa*, p. 123.

[2] *Complevi in Cusa* 1440 *XII Februarii*, is the note in Nicholas's own hand in his own copy of the book (i.e. *cod*. E. 2.). Uebinger, *Die philosophischen Schriften des Nikolaus Cusanus*, in *Zeitschrift für Philosophie*, 103, p. 80 ; Scharpff, *Reformator*, p. 111.

[3] Uebinger would date it from 1440. *Zeitschrift für Philosophie*, 103, p. 65.

[4] The manuscript is dated : 1445, *Moguncie*. Vansteenberghe, *Nicolas de Cues*, p. 269.

[5] It is mentioned in the *Apologia*, and was therefore written before 1449. The manuscripts place it between the *De filiatione Dei* and the *De Genesi*. Gerard had been auxiliary

latter tract is dedicated to *Gerardus, Episcopus Sol-onensis*, apparently Salona, a see suffragan of that of Athens. Gerard was a Franciscan and a Bishop *in partibus*. The *De filiatione Dei* [1] dates from 1445, and the *De genesi* from 1447.[2] The former was written on the suggestion of Conrad of Wart-burg, a canon of Münster, and a friend of Nicho-las's. The latter, written at Liége, is a dialogue between Nicholas and a certain Conrad, without doubt the person just mentioned. The *Apologia doctae ignorantiae* dates from October 1449,[3] and was written in reply to the charge of heresy advanced by Wenck of Heidelberg, in his *De ignota litteratura*. Johannes Wenck of Herrenberg was professor of theology at Heidelberg, and rector of the theological faculty there in 1435, 1444 and 1451. He found in the work of Nicholas what he regarded as the errors of the Waldenses and the Beghards, and he extracted from it thirty-seven propositions which he deemed heretical.[4] Wenck was a strong parti-san of the Council of Basel, and this lent him an animus in his attack upon Nicholas.[5] The *Apologia*,

bishop at Trèves from 1441 to 1445, which explains the acquaintance with Nicholas. Rotta, *Il Cardinale Nicolò di Cusa*, p. 228.

[1] It is dedicated to *Conrado Vuartobergensi, Canonico monasterii Memphelti, denoto sacerdoti.*

[2] The manuscript is dated: *Finitum anno 1447, 2ª marcii, Leodi.*

[3] Uebinger, in *Zeitschrift für Philosophie*, 103, p. 65. Van-steenberghe, *Nicolas de Cues*, p. 271.

[4] See the text of the *De ignota litteratura*, printed by Van-steenberghe in *Beiträge zur Geschichte der Philosophie des Mittelalters*, Bd. viii, Hft. 6, pp. 21, 30.

[5] Nicholas refers to Wenck's conciliar bias in *Apologia*, p. 64.

strangely enough, is more of a difficulty to those
who are concerned about Nicholas's orthodoxy
than the work it was written to defend, for it
commends the writings of Eckhart, which were
always suspect, and those of Scotus Erigena (whom
Nicholas calls Scotigena) and of his followers,
Amalric of Bena and David of Dinant,[1] which
had been expressly condemned by the Church.
It was believed by Erdmann [2] that the *Apologia*
was written by a disciple of Nicholas, mainly on
the ground of the praise which is lavished on the
Cusan philosophy. It is to be observed, however, that the praise is of the ideas of the *De docta
ignorantia*, rather than of the writer, and that it is
no more exaggerated in the *Apologia* than in the
Idiota.

Next in order of time are four dialogues, which
were written about a year after the *Apologia*. The
first, the *De sapientia*, is in two books, which are
dated respectively, Rieti, the 1st of July, and
Fabriano, the 7th and 8th of August 1450.[3]
The *De mente* was finished at the Camaldulensian
monastery in the Val de Castro, near Fabriano,
on the 23rd of August,[4] and the *De staticis experimentis* at Fabriano, on the 14th of Septem-

[1] *Apologia*, pp. 70-3.

[2] *Geschichte der Philosophie*, i, p. 444.

[3] Uebinger, in *Zeitschrift für Philosophie*, 103, p. 66.

[4] The manuscript is dated : *In monasterio vallis castri ordinis
camaldulensis ubi S. Romualdus, caput ordinis, sepultus est, prope
Fabrianum in marchia anchonitana anno d.* 1450, *die* 23 *Aug.
finivi hunc conceptum de mente. Nicolaus Card. S. Petri ad
vincula.* Scharpff, *Reformator*, p. 164.

This is the famous abbey and hermitage of Camaldoli,
mentioned by Dante (*Purgatorio*, v, 96).

ber.[1] These four little books, all written in the year 1450, and within three months, are classed together as the *Idiota*, because in each of them one of the principal interlocutors is the 'idiot'— the 'simple man'.

Next in date is the tract called *De novissimis diebus*, written in 1452, or 1453 [2]—a curious little work which fixes the date of the end of the world as early in the eighteenth century. Nicholas calculates that there were thirty-four jubilees, or 1,700 years, between Adam and the Deluge (deriving the date of the latter event from Philo); [3] a similar period between the Deluge and Moses; a similar period between Moses and Christ; and then concludes that another period of 1,700 years will elapse between either the birth or the death of our Lord and the end of the world. This is linked up with the doctrine of the ages of the world, which Nicholas found in Erigena and in Augustine,[4] and the conclusion is that the Second Advent and the overthrow of Antichrist will come to pass within the first thirty-four years of the eighteenth century.[5] Three other of Nicholas's smaller writ-

---

[1] The manuscript is dated: *Anno dom.* 1450, *die* 14 *Sept. Fabriani complevi de staticis experimentis—Nicolaus Card. S. Petri ad vincula.* See Scharpff, *Reformator*, p. 165.

[2] Uebinger, in *Zeitschrift für Philosophie*, 103, p. 66.

[3] He had a manuscript of Philo's work *In Genesim* in his library. Marx, *Verzeichnis*, p. 11.

[4] *De divisione naturae* (1020.–1021. A, Col. 122, ed. Migne). Augustine, *De civ. Dei*, xxiii, p. 30.

[5] The Second Advent is elsewhere described as fourfold —in the flesh; spiritual and sacramental; in the clouds; and finally to Judgement. *Excit.*, iii (*Dicite filiae Zion*), p. 423. In the passage about the Second Advent in the *De*

ings belong to the year 1453, the *Complementum theologicum*,[1] the *De pace seu concordantia fidei*,[2] and the *De visione Dei*. The latter was sent to Nicholas's admiring friends, the Benedictines of Tegernsee, and dedicated to the Abbot.

Next in date, and closely akin in subject, is the *De beryllo*, which was finished on the 18th of August 1458, at Buchenstein.[3]   The important dialogue

docta ignorantia, iii, 11, p. 58, *quasi per nubem rationem*, the reading should be *rariorem*.

[1] In a letter to the Abbot and the monks of Tegernsee, dated 14th September 1453, he writes—Scripsi hiis diebus *De mathematicis complementis* libellum ad S. d. Nicolaum papam, qui rarissimus est, nam omnia actenus incognita manifestat in mathematicis ; cui libello adiunxi alium *De theologicis complementis*, in quo transtuli mathematicas figuras ad theologicalem infinitatem.

He sent the *De mathematicis complementis* to Tegernsee on the 12th of February 1454. Vansteenberghe, *Autour de la docte Ignorance*, in *Beiträge zur Geschichte der Philosophie des Mittelalters*, Bd. xiv, Hft. 2-4, pp. 116, 122.

[2] This work takes the form of a discussion between interlocutors of different nationalities, a Jew, a Greek, an Italian, a Turk, and so on.   Possibly the form was suggested by Raymond Lull's work, *The Book of the Heathen and the Three Sages*, which is a discussion between a Jew, a Christian, a Mohammedan, and a heathen.

[3] We know from letters of the 16th of August 1454 that he was then at work on the *De beryllo*.   In a letter of the 9th of January 1456, to Caspar Ainsdorfer, the Abbot, he promises to send it, with some of his sermons, to the monks of Tegernsee. Vansteenberghe, *Autour de la docte Ignorance*, in *Beiträge zur Geschichte der Philosophie des Mittelalters*, Bd. xiv, Hft. 2-4, pp. 139-40, 162.

The tract was not completed until 1458.   The manuscript bears the inscription : 1458.   18 Augusti in castro Sancti Raphaelis, and there is added, in another hand, the note : alio vocabulo dicto Boethensteyn (Kraus, *Handschriften-Sammlung*, p. 40).   This means Buchenstein.

entitled *De Possest* was probably composed at Andraz, early in 1460. The interlocutors are Nicholas himself, Bernard Kraiburg,[1] and the Cardinal's former secretary, John Andrew Bussi.[2]

The dialogue *De non aliud*,[3] written at Rome early in 1462, introduces, beside the Cardinal and Bussi, Peter Balbus, of Pisa, who became a few years later Bishop of Tropea,[4] and Ferdinand Martin,

---

[1] Bernard, born at Kraiburg on the Inn, was Chancellor of the archdiocese of Salzburg. He wrote, in defence of Nicholas, a tract entitled : *Narratio rei gestae per Sigismundum, Duc. Austr. contra Cardinalem de Cusa.*

When the diocese of Brixen was under the interdict, Bernard was appointed by the Pope to administer it, but declined the office, at the wish of his superior, the Archbishop of Salzburg. Bernard was Bishop of Chiemsee from 1467 until his death ten years later. Rotta, in his introduction to the *De docta ignorantia*, is mistaken (like Scharpff, whom he follows) in thinking that the *Bernardus* of the dialogue is Bernard the Prior of Tegernsee.

[2] Bishop of Accia in 1463, and of Aleria in 1466.

[3] This is one of the works which Lefèvre lamented that he could not find. It was discovered and published by Dr. Uebinger, as an appendix to his work *Die Gotteslehre des Nikolaus Cusanus.* The existence of such a work was known from a reference in the *De venatione sapientiae*, xiv, p. 309 : Scripsi autem latius *de non aliud* in dialogo quadri-locutorio. Dr. Uebinger discovered it in the Hof- und Staatsbibliothek at Munich (No. 24848). The manuscript is the work of the Nuremberg humanist, Hartmann Schedel and dates from 1496, as we learn from the conclusion : Scripsi Hartmannus Schedel, artium et utriusque medicinae doctor, anno domini 1496 die 6 mensis Aprilis Nurembergae. Uebinger, *Die Gotteslehre*, pp. 140–1.

[4] He was a native of Pisa, and had been a fellow-student of Nicholas at Padua. He dedicated to the Cardinal his translation of Alcinoüs' *Epitome of Plato.* He died at Rome in 1479. Uebinger, *Die Gotteslehre*, p. 142.

of Roritz, a Portuguese who was Nicholas's physician.[1]

[1] *Ferdinandus Matim, Portugallensis natione.* Uebinger conjectured that *Matim* should be *Martini* (Ibid., p. 142), but he did not at the time identify this interlocutor with the *Fernandus de Roritz, canonicus Ulixponensis,* who was one of the witnesses of Nicholas's will. In the latter years of the Cardinal's life, Ferdinand was his physician. On the 23rd of December 1462, Simon Wehlen, Nicholas's nephew, wrote from Venice to M. *Ferdinando, arcium doctori, physico card. S. Petri.* There can be no doubt as to the identification.

Martins (this is the Portuguese form of the name) has a special interest as being the link between Toscanelli and Columbus in a correspondence that probably had a profound influence upon the discovery of America. C. R. Markham, *The Journal of Columbus,* p. 111. Columbus wrote to Toscanelli, the most celebrated physicist of the time, to obtain confirmation of his theories as to a westward voyage to India. He had heard of a letter that Toscanelli had written to Martins, in response to the request of King Alfonso. This letter is dated 25th June 1474 (the text of it is in Vignaud, *Toscanelli and Columbus,* pp. 294–303).

Through Lorenzo Geraldi, he secured a copy of it from Toscanelli, who addressed a few words to Columbus himself at the beginning and end of it. Along with the letter he sent a map. (This is lost; there is a conjectural reconstruction of it in Winson's *Narrative and Critical History of America.*) We know that it showed, on one side, all the coasts from Ireland to Guinea, with the islands, and on the other side, the continent and isles of the Indies, with the distances which must be traversed to reach them. C. R. Markham, *Life of Columbus,* p. 31. The letter explains that the chart was divided by meridian lines into equal spaces of 150 miles; there were twenty-six such spaces, or 3,900 miles, between Lisbon and the famous city of Quisai (Marco Polo's Quinsay) now Hangchau, south of Shanghai; while ten spaces, or 1,500 miles, separated the island of Antilia (one of the fabled islands of the Mare Tenebrosum) from Cipango or Japan—whence Toscanelli's encouraging con-

Early in the following year, Nicholas read the *De vitis philosophorum* of Diogenes Laertius, and this determined him to recapitulate, in a short work, those of his own thoughts that he judged most vital and valuable. The result was the *De venatione*

clusion that ' the spaces of the sea to be crossed to the unknown parts are not large '. This communication undoubtedly deepened Columbus's faith in his own judgement. Toscanelli's descriptions of Quinsay, *nobilissima et maxima civitas, et nomen eius sonat cita del cielo, civitas coeli, et multa miranda de ea narrantur*, and of Cipango, *insula fertillisima auro, margaritis et gemmis*, are derived from Marco Polo.

On his return from his memorable voyage, Columbus wrote to Toscanelli, now very aged, telling him of the discovery he had made. C. R. Markham, *Life of Columbus*, p. 134.

The French scholar Henri Vignaud (in his *Histoire critique de la grande entreprise de Christophe Colombe*, and his English work, *Toscanelli and Columbus*) has endeavoured to prove (with much ingenuity and learning) that the correspondence is a forgery. Incidentally he denies that the Ferdinand de Roritz, who was one of the witnesses of the will of Nicholas, is the same person as the Ferdinand Martins to whom Toscanelli's letter is addressed. But that there should be, among the immediate friends of Toscanelli and Nicholas, *two* persons who were *both* of Portuguese nationality, who were *both* named Ferdinand, and who were *both* Canons of Lisbon, is too much of a coincidence to be believed. There is not the slightest doubt that the *Fernandus de Roritz, canonicus Ulixponensis* who witnessed Nicholas's will, the *Ferdinandus Martini canonicus Ulyssiponensi*, to whom Toscanelli's letter was addressed, the *Ferdinandus Matim, Portugallensis natione*, who is one of the interlocutors in the *De non aliud*, and the *Magister Ferdinandus, artium doctor*, who was the Cardinal's physician, are one and the same person. See the authorities mentioned in the text, Uzielli, *La vita e i tempi di Paolo dal Pozzo Toscanelli*, pp. 583, 658, and Vansteenberghe, *Nicolas de Cues*, pp. 252, 274.

sapientiae.[1]   Three other small works belong to the year 1463, the *De apice theoriae*, the *De ludo globi* and the *Compendium*.[2] The first is a dialogue between Nicholas and Peter Erkelenz, his secretary, who was a Canon of Aix-la-Chapelle. The second consists of two dialogues, written at Rome, in the autumn of the year. The former dialogue is between Nicholas and John, the son of Otho, the Count Palatine of the Rhine ; the second is between Nicholas and Albert, the son of Albert III of Bavaria. The *Compendium* seems to have been written late in the year, and is, as the name implies, a summary of the Cusan doctrines, and also an introduction to the Cardinal's other works.

For many years of his life Nicholas had been deeply interested in Islam, and deeply concerned, as all thinking men were in those days, at the threatening advance of the Turks in the East of Europe. At the Council of Basel he procured a copy of the translation of the Koran, made at the instance of Peter of Clugny three hundred years before.[3] He made there, also, the acquaintance of John of Segovia, who, as a Spaniard, was more

[1] See the Prologue.   Cf. Uebinger, *Die Gotteslehre*, p. 70 ; Vansteenberghe, *Nicolas de Cues*, p. 274.

[2] Vansteenberghe thinks, with some reason, that the *De apice theoriae* was written last, and sees in it ' le testament spirituel du Cardinal ' (p. 275). Uebinger remarks in *Die Gotteslehre* (p. 127) ' dass die beiden Gespräche *De ludo globi* nach ganz unzweideutigen inneren und äusseren Zeugnissen in das Jahr 1464, höchstwahrscheinlich in den März dieses Jahres, fallen.'

[3] It is still in the library at Cues. The manuscript is annotated in the hand of Nicholas. Marx, *Verzeichnis*, p. 108.

or less familiar with the religion of the Moors.[1]
A little later, on his visit to Constantinople, he
found at the Dominican Convent in Pera another
copy of the translation of the Koran which he
already possessed,[2] and at the Franciscan Convent
of the Holy Cross a manuscript of the original
Arabic, which the friars explained to him.[3] He
also discovered that John of Damascus had written
against Mahometanism, and possessed himself of
these writings—a section of the $\Pi\epsilon\varrho\grave{\iota}$ $A\acute{\iota}\varrho\acute{\epsilon}\sigma\epsilon\omega\nu$,
and the two dialogues ($\Delta\iota\acute{\alpha}\lambda\epsilon\xi\iota\varsigma$ $\Sigma\alpha\varrho\varrho\alpha\varkappa\acute{\eta}\nu\upsilon$ $\varkappa\alpha\grave{\iota}$
$X\varrho\iota\sigma\tau\iota\alpha\nu\upsilon\tilde{\upsilon}$)[4] between a Saracen and a Christian.

Later still, when the disastrous victories of the
Turks at Varna and Kossovo emphasized the
Mahometan menace, he urged his friend Denys the
Carthusian to write against Islam, and the monk
wrote his tract *Contra perfidiam Mahometi*, and
dedicated it to the Cardinal.[5]

Constantinople fell on the 29th of May 1453, and
a shudder of apprehension and pity went through
Christendom. The Pope organized a Crusade
against the victorious Turks, and charged Nicholas
in September 1455 with a mission to the whole of
Germany and England to further it.[6] Nicholas
did not leave his diocese, where he was detained
by his contest with Sigismund. By the summer of
1456 the victorious Turks were approaching the
Danube, and Rome was in despair. On the 14th

[1] Vansteenberghe, *Nicolas de Cues*, p. 228.
[2] *De cribr. Alchorani*, (Prologue) p. 879.
[3] Scharpff, *Reformator*, p. 113.
[4] In Migne, *Patrologia Graeca*, vol. 94 (764–74), and vol.
96 (1335–48).
[5] Vansteenberghe, *Nicolas de Cues*, p. 228.
[6] Ibid., p. 231.

of July John Hunyadi won a brilliant victory under the walls of Belgrade, utterly defeating 40,000 Turks, and Christendom breathed once more.

The Pope requested Nicholas to write a refutation of the errors of Islam, and the *Cribratio Alchorani* was the result. It was probably written late in 1460 or early in 1461.[1] The most striking fact about the book is the constructive method of it. Nicholas is not content, as his few predecessors in the field had been, with defining and denouncing the errors of Islam. He attempts to sift out the truth which is found in the Koran, and then to demonstrate, on this basis, the truth of Christianity.[2] He makes the historical point that Mahomet's misrepresentations of the Christian religion are largely due to the fact that he only knew it in the perverted form of Nestorianism—an argument that is capable of a much wider and more drastic application than Nicholas dreamt, and not in respect of Islam only. It illustrates Nicholas's candour of mind that he frankly recognizes the literary merit of the Koran.[3]

[1] Vansteenberghe, *Nicolas de Cues*, p. 233.

[2] He says, in the Prologue, *Ego ingenium applicui, ut etiam ex Alchoran Evangelium verum ostenderem* (p. 880). But this in no way hinders him from identifying Mahomet with one of the monsters of the Apocalypse. Primam bestiam, de aqua seu mari ascendentem, possumus Mahumet intelligere, cuius nomen ex מים, hoc est aqua ortum est. *Excit.*, vii (*Iterum venturus est iudicare*), p. 560.

[3] *De Cribr. Alchorani*, p. 886.

III

THE PHILOSOPHY OF NICHOLAS OF CUSA

CHAPTER I

GENERAL PRINCIPLES

THE large place to which Nicholas of Cusa is entitled in the history of philosophical thought has never been sufficiently recognized. There is, perhaps, no thinker of such real importance and of such wide influence who has been so singularly neglected. He has not been undervalued, as a rule, by those who have studied him, but those who have studied him closely have been few. There are many reasons for this neglect. The most potent, perhaps, is the fact that Nicholas lived precisely when he did, with the result of that upon his intellectual position. He presents a genuine difficulty to our modern instinct for classification. He lived at a period which might be regarded with equal truth as the very end of the Middle Ages, or as the very beginning of the Renaissance. That particular generation was a dubious link between the medieval and the modern world, and the date is reflected in the doctrine of Nicholas. In one sense it is the oblique result of both the scholasticism and the mysticism of the thirteenth and fourteenth centuries; in another sense it is the uncertain prelude of the humanism of the fifteenth and sixteenth centuries.[1] Nicholas of Cusa stands on the disputed confines [2] of two different eras, ' betwixt two worlds, One dead, the other powerless to be born '.

Then there are practical difficulties of a very considerable kind in the way of any serious study of Nicholas's system. For ordinary purposes there are only two approximately complete editions of his works, both dating from the sixteenth century,[3] and both extremely scarce. There is a great deal of critical work yet to be done before we can hope to possess a really satisfactory text. The typography is naturally archaic, in some places simply swarming in contractions; and the punctuation is frequently misleading. Then the style of Nicholas is difficult and barbarous; his thought is often extremely abstract and paradoxical; many of his definitions are exceedingly inadequate; and he employs a philosophical vocabulary which is (to quote the heartfelt cry of a French savant) *d'une instabilité déconcertante*.[4] Excepting a few monographs by

[1] Windelband, *Die Geschichte der neueren Philosophie*, i, p. 45; De Wulf, *Histoire de la philosophie médiévale*, p. 486; J. Ritter, *Docta Ignorantia, die Theorie des Nichtwissens bei Nicolaus Cusanus*, p. 7.

[2] Falckenberg, *Grundzüge der Philosophie des Nicolaus Cusanus*, p. 3.

[3] The Paris edition of 1514, edited by Faber Stapulensis, and the Basel edition of 1565, edited by Henri Petri.

There is a useful modern edition of the *De docta ignorantia*, by Dr. Paolo Rotta, with Italian notes (Bari, 1913), but though there has been a collation of the principal manuscripts, and various readings are given, it is by no means a critical edition of the text.

[4] Vansteenberghe, *Nicolas de Cues*, p. 349.

German and Italian scholars [1] there is very little expository literature dealing with the philosophy of Nicholas. The cumulative effect of all this is to make the study of the Cusan system, at first hand, an enterprise that demands some courage.

The whole form of Nicholas's philosophy, we would suggest, was determined by the fact that a mind which was equally characterized by philosophical subtlety and by mathematical precision was dominated also by a passion for unity. The monistic and optimistic character of his doctrine both illustrate this; he was impatient of the opposition of infinite and finite, of thought and being, of good and evil. He persistently tried to see all things under one final aspect, and to express all truth in one ultimate formula. Not only so: he desired to make that formula as exact and irrefutable as an equation in mathematics. He seems to have believed that he had attained that convincing and conquering finality, both in thought and language, and that there really was a prospect of uniting all the differing faiths and philosophies of the world on the basis of his subtle abstractions.

In this connexion, neither the state of the world in which he lived nor his own share in ecclesiastical affairs should be forgotten. He had seen great schisms in the Church; he could remember the time when there had been three Popes, each claiming to be the Vicar of Christ, and he had done much himself to restore Christendom to a single obedience; he had been brought into close contact with the Hussite movement, he had been brought

[1] Particularly those of Scharpff, Falckenberg, Uebinger, and Rotta.

into equally intimate connexion with the Orthodox Church, and he had done his best to reconcile both the Bohemians and the Greeks, and to reunite them both with Rome. He had also been in intellectual contact with Islam, and was deeply concerned to seek methods of reconciliation with that faith. His whole ecclesiastical career, in fact, had been an apostolate of unity. It is not fanciful, perhaps, to see this reflected in his thought, with its persistent reconciliation of contradictions, and its unitary bias throughout.

The system of Nicholas takes its departure, as far as essential metaphysics are concerned, from the Neoplatonist view of God and the world,[1] which he had inherited from Eckhart, Erigena, and the pseudo-Dionysius. That view was profoundly modified in the Cardinal's speculations, but there can be no doubt that it lies at the beginning and at the base of his philosophy. Neoplatonism conceived of God as essential, eternal unity, utterly bare of all distinction or differentiation, and was then faced with the difficulty of getting from that unity to the multiplicity and difference and change of the phenomenal world. Hence the κόσμος νοητός, the emanations, the aeons, the intermediate existences which are characteristic of the different forms of Neoplatonism and of Gnosticism. Hence, too, the θεῖα θελήματα of Dionysius and the *causae primordiales* of Erigena (though the Scot escapes much of the difficulty by the large place which the doctrine of the Trinity holds in his scheme of thought—a point on which he particu-

[1] R. Eucken, *Nicolaus von Cues*, in *Philosophische Monatshefte*, Bd. xiv (1878), pp. 450, 468.

larly influenced Nicholas). This marked tendency to bridge the gulf between the one and the many by the device of intermediate powers which are regarded as in some sense both created and creative, is one of the distinct characteristics of Neoplatonism, and it is interesting to note that it is quite distinctly foreshadowed in the *Timaeus*.

Nicholas overcomes the difficulty in a way that is both more subtle and more courageous. He boldly identifies the opposite terms, at any rate for the purpose of his ultimate metaphysics. It is as if reality has two sides, of which one is God, the invisible and ultimate reality, and the other is the world, the visible and derived reality.[1] Reality, as originative and communicative, is God; as originated and communicated, it is the world. All is in God, as uncreated; all is in the world, as created.[2] Thus the existence of God involves the existence of the world, and gives it finite actuality. And equally the existence of the world involves the existence of God, and gives it finite actuality. For God is God, as existing infinitely, and God is the Universe, as existing finitely. The finite is implicit in the infinite, the infinite is explicit in the finite. The very fact of the multiplicity and finiteness of the world postulates the existence of the One and the Infinite.[3] And the very notion of Unity and Infinity involves the possibility of the multiple

---

[1] Quid est mundus, nisi invisibilis Dei apparitio? quid Deus, nisi visibilium invisibilitas? *De Possest*, p. 266.

[2] Idem ipsum Deus et creatura: secundum modum datoris Deus, secundum modum dati creatura. *De dato*, ii, p. 286. Cf. *De Possest*, p. 265.

[3] Multitudo unitatem praesupponit. *De Crib. Alch.*, ii, 7, p. 901. Cf. *De ven. sap.*, xxi, p. 314.

8

and the finite, and more than the possibility, since possibility and actuality are one in God. God and the universe are thus strictly correlative terms; each involves the other. God is prior to the actuality which is distinguished from possibility, and prior to the possibility which is distinguished from actuality.[1] Every possibility, therefore, must exist, and the existence of God necessitates the existence of the world as strictly as the existence of the world necessitates the existence of God, though the necessity is not of the same order, for in the one case it is real and absolute, and in the other it is logical and relative. That is to say, the being of the universe derives from God, but the being of God does not derive from the universe.[2] Yet, if God is, the world must be, for the very character of the existence of God is that it is creative; and if the world is, God must be, for the very character of the existence of the world is that it is created.

The relation may be illustrated by the double conception of motion and rest, which is, indeed, one of the illustrations which Nicholas uses, or rather one of the aspects under which he sees the

[1] Deus est ante differentiam actus et potentiae. *De ven. sap.*, xxix, p. 322. Cf. *De Possest*, p. 251.

[2] This is precisely Eckhart's doctrine. Got ist wesen, und wesen ist niht got. Jostes, *Meister Eckhart und seine Jünger*, p. 85. So, also, in Spinoza's doctrine of essence. 'While defining participation of essence to involve reciprocal conditioning, he expressly denies that this degree of unity exists between God and particular beings. God is *sine qua non* to them, but they are not *sine quibus non* to Him.' B. Bosanquet, *The Meeting of Extremes in Contemporary Philosophy*, p. 92.

problem, for it must be remembered that with him all these minor antitheses and antinomies in the world are actually resolved by the principle of the coincidence of contraries. Rest and motion imply each other; it is impossible to conceive of one except as the opposite of the other, and the existence of the one necessarily implies at least the possibility of the existence of the other. All motion begins from rest, and ends in rest. Therefore motion is implicit in rest, and rest is explicit in motion. Rest is prior to motion, for rest is the unoriginated, the undifferentiated condition, the eternal state; but it contains motion within itself, the whole possibility of motion, and indeed the whole actuality of it, for possibility and actuality are one in the eternal unity. Rest is the eternal possibility of the actuality of temporal motion, and the eternal actuality of the possibility of temporal motion.

And so precisely with God and the world. All begins from God, and all ends in God, as motion begins from rest, and ends in rest. God is all of all that is, and yet nothing of all that is.[1] He is

---

[1] Omnia, et nihil omnium. *De doct. ign.*, i, 16, p. 11. Cf. *Excit.*, vii (*Ubi est qui natus est rex Iudaeorum*), p. 570. Compare the language of Eckhart: Got ist in allen dingen. Ie mer er ist in den dingen, ie mer ist er uz den dingen: ie me er inne, ie mer er uze ist. Pfeiffer, *Meister Eckhart*, p. 206. Got also ist in allen dingen, daz er alzemale ist uz allen dingen. Ist danne eteswa ein kreature mit gebrechlicheit, und wan danne got alzemale ist uzerund der kreature, darumbe so mac in der gebreche niht berüeren. Ibid., p. 612. The Latin of this last passage, as recovered by Denifle, is: Deus sic totus in quolibet, quod totus est extra quodlibet, et propter hoc ea, que sunt cuiuslibet, ipsi non con-

all that is, in unity and perfection, but nothing that is, in limitation and multiplicity.[1] Everything that exists is implicit in God, and explicit in the universe. God is the unoriginated, undifferentiated ground of all possibility and all actuality, and these are one in Him.[2] The universe is the evolution of limited possibility into limited actuality, which becomes manifold in the process, for multiplicity is the very character of the finite, as unity is the very character of the infinite. And so multiplicity arises out of unity. Within the field of our own knowledge we know many individual things as belonging to one kind, and hence number arises. That is to say, multiplicity depends upon unity, for if we had not the notion of one kind to which many things belong, we could not have the notion of things as many. Thus the multiplicity of things in the universe arises out of the unity of God, in which the many is one. Without number there could be no multiplicity of things, for without number there can be no separation or order or proportion. Unity itself is not number, but it is the principle of number, as the minimum, and the end of number, as the maximum. Things

veniunt, puta variari, senescere aut corrumpi. Denifle, *Meister Eckeharts lateinische Schriften*, in *Archiv für Litteratur- und Kirchengeschichte des Mittelalters*, ii, p. 432.

[1] This again is Eckhart's doctrine : Got hat alliu dinc verborgenliche in ime selber, aber niht diz noch daz nach underscheide, sunder ein nach der einikeit. Pfeiffer, *Meister Eckhart*, p. 333. Cf. Lenz, *Die docta ignorantia des Nikolaus Cusanus*, p. 58.

[2] Solus Deus est possest, quia est actu, quod esse potest. *De ven. sap.*, xiii, p. 307. Cf. Rossi, *Niccolò di Cusa e la direzione monistica della filosofia del Rinascimento*, pp. 45-6.

are different, because God in eternity has thought of them differently, and thence multiplicity arises, though in Him the difference is identity and the multiplicity is unity. But how are we to conceive that multiplicity in unity? Manifestly not as the multiplicity of individuals in a species, or the multiplicity of species in a genus, where the species and the genus are both abstractions. The unity of all in God is not an abstraction of the reason, neither is it a mingling of the many into one. Conceive things without God, and they are nothing. Conceive God without things, and He is, and they are nothing. Conceive God in so far as He is in things, and you are at once in error, for you represent to yourself that things are entities in which God is, but the being of a thing is not in itself, as something separate; the thing has its being from God. (Strictly it is not being in the primary sense, so that it is not being of a kind, so to speak, in which God could be, for the very nature of it is derived and dependent and secondary : it is not *esse*, but *abesse*.) [1] Finally conceive things, in so far as they are in God, and then you hold at the same time the thought of the unity of God, and of the multiplicity of things, and of that created multiplicity as one in the uncreated unity. [2]

The constant emphasis upon number is very characteristic of Nicholas, and this is one of the points at which he exhibits such high regard for

---

[1] Esse rei non est aliud, ut est diversa res, sed eius esse est abesse. *De doct. ign.*, ii, 3, p. 27. The printed editions wrongly read *aliquid* for *aliud*, and *a maximi esse* for *abesse*. See Uebinger, *Die Gotteslehre des Nikolaus Cusanus*, p. 48.

[2] *De doct. ign.*, ii, 3, p. 27.

what he knew of Pythagorean doctrine,[1] which naturally made a special appeal to his mathematical mind. Unity is not number, but it is the beginning of number. Though number has a beginning it has no end, and it thus possesses a kind of qualified infinity. There are many particular applications of this doctrine. Thus number is the measure of duration, and so time has its measure from number but its source in eternity. It is an image of eternity, with a beginning but without an end—a sentence which recalls Plato's great phrase.[2] And so the finite existence of the world has a beginning, yet the essential being of the world is eternity.[3] Thus unity, eternity, and being, which are the same, are the source and principle of number, of time, and of existence, though unity is not number, and eternity is not time, and absolute being is not finite existence.

Since God is pure unity, absolutely bare of all differentiation, all the divine attributes coincide. All that may truly be said of God, though separated into different conceptions in our minds, is one and the same truth in His immutable nature. Hence all theology moves in a circle.[4] The being of God, the will of God, the act of God, are absolutely one and identical ; these conceptions are merely the different names by which we distinguish the different aspects in which our minds see the one, eternal,

---

[1] *De doct. ign.*, i, 11, p. 8 ; *De ludo globi*, ii, p. 236.
[2] *Timaeus*, 37. d.
[3] *De dato*, iii, p. 288.
[4] Omnis theologia circularis et in circulo posita existit. *De doct. ign.*, i, 21, p. 17. Tota theologia in circulo posita dicitur. *De vis. Dei*, iii, p. 183.

immutable essence of God. This is also the express doctrine of Augustine, Erigena, and Eckhart.[1]

There is some development in Nicholas's doctrine of God as we pass from his earlier to his later works, but it is a development in nomenclature and emphasis rather than in thought. He began with a conception of God as the superessential Unity, which is opposed to no otherness, and in which all contraries coincide. He never really departed from that position. But he came more and more in later life to use phrases which stress the self-identity of the Godhead. God is *Idem*,[2] for unity, infinity, actuality, possibility, existence, nothingness, all that can be thought, all that surpasses thought, is the same in Him. He is *Non Aliud*,[3] for there is nothing to which He is other,[4] since He is unrelated and unconditioned and absolute. He is the *Possest*,[5] because in Him possibility (*posse*) and actuality (*est*) are one. It can hardly be said that there is any real advance in thought

---

[1] Augustine, *De civ. Dei*, viii, 6 ; Erigena, *De div. nat.*, iii, 17 (674, A, vol. 122, ed. Migne) ; Pfeiffer, *Meister Eckhart*, p. 287. Cf. St. Thomas Aquinas, *Summa theol.*, i, qu. 19, art. 1.

[2] Tu vero concipito Idem absolute, supra idem in vocabulo considerabile. *De Genesi*, p. 128. Cf. Ranft, *Schöpfer und Geschöpf nach Kardinal Nikolaus von Cusa*, pp. 78–9.

[3] *De non aliud*, in Uebinger, *Gotteslehre*, p. 155.

[4] The germ of this doctrine is in Erigena and Eckhart. Est enim Deus similium similitudo, et dissimilitudo dissimilium, oppositorum oppositio, et contrariorum contrarietas. *De div. nat.*, i, 72 (517, B, vol. 122, ed. Migne). Got der ist ein versagen dez versagens : daz ein daz verseit alle anderheit. Jostes, *Meister Eckhart und seine Jünger*, p. 7.

[5] *De Possest*, p. 252.

here; the notion of the changeless identity of the Deity is really involved in the conception, found in Nicholas's earliest books, of God as immutable Unity. But Nicholas came, in later life, to use new terms which stress the internal identity, so to speak, rather than the universal inclusiveness of the Absolute, and at the same time he came to emphasize the dynamic rather than the static aspect of the conception.

It follows necessarily from the conception of the nature of God held by our philosopher that the creation of the universe is thought of rather as a process in the life of God than as a separate act of His will, though Nicholas does attribute it, in express phrases, to the will of God, in more than one of his writings.[1]   But if to be, to think, to will, to act, to see, to speak, are all one in God,[2] the world is naturally envisaged rather as a necessary emanation from the nature of God than as an arbitrary product of the will of God.   As Nicholas himself says, with God to see is to create, and He sees nothing but Himself: how then can He create what is not Himself?[3]   (The question of eternal or temporal creation hardly arises, for Nicholas held, like Augustine, that time only comes into being along with the world.)[4]   The creation is a necessary consequence of the nature of God, but Nicholas and many of the mystics would have

[1] *De genesi*, p. 131;   *Excit.*, iii (*Verbum caro factum est*), p. 418.

[2] *Excit.*, viii (*Multifariae*), p. 620.

[3] *De vis. Dei*, xii, p. 192.   Cf. Erigena, *De div. nat.*, i, 12, iii, 17 (455, B, 674, A, vol. 122, ed. Migne).

[4] *Excit.*, vii (*Induimini Dominum Iesum Christum*), p. 558.

contended that it is none the less a free act of God.
The necessity is a moral necessity ; it is not an
external constraint. God, being what He is,
must create, because essential goodness is originative, expansive, communicative, creative, in its
very nature.[1] But the nature of God is not to
be separated from His will, since all aspects and
attributes are one in Him, and it is of the essence
of the will of God that it should be free.[2] It
would not be a will if it were not free. So that
the creation is really an act, and a free act, of the
will of God, no less than a necessary consequence
of His nature.[3]

Fiorentino has called Nicholas, rather happily,
*l'ultimo dei mistici tedeschi ed il primo dei filosofi di
quella nazione,*[4] and there can be no doubt that
he is as much a mystic as a philosopher in his ultimate doctrines. His whole view of the relation
between God and the universe is a development
of the conception, partly Neoplatonist in origin,
which we associate with the mystics. The fundamental position is that all existence must derive
from God, and that not arbitrarily, as by a casual
act of will, but organically, by a necessity which lies
deep in the nature of God. But it is a free necessity, and a moral necessity, for though it results
inevitably from the nature of God, it is still an
act of the will of God, an act of the mind of God,
though these are not separate motions, but are
one in Him. Now this implies purpose, design,

[1] *Excit.*, v (*Pax hominibus*), p. 498.
[2] *Excit.*, v (*Caelum et terra*), p. 494.
[3] Cf. Rothe, *Dogmatik*, pp. 143-4.
[4] *Rinascimento filosofico nel quattrocento*, p. 111.

thought, and we are compelled to think of all things as being in the thought of God before they exist phenomenally. As Augustine said, God does not know things because they are, but things are because God knows them.[1] That is, the thought of things in the mind of God is not reflective and representative, as in the mind of man, but creative and constitutive. The finite form of the thing gives it individuality, and separates it to that extent from God and from all else, as an individual existence, but the real essence of the thing, without which it would not be at all, lies in the thought of God. Therefore all things in God are God; the essence of them, as being in the thought of God, is one with God.

Now all this is characteristic mysticism of the type which prevailed among the Dominicans in Germany. Perhaps the main difference of emphasis in Nicholas is that he stressed more than most mystics, and vastly more than Eckhart, for example, the real individuality of things. He teaches, like the mystics, that as things become temporal and multiple and finite, they fall away from God, as lapsing more and more from the one, the eternal, the infinite. But he teaches also that it is by this very process of becoming individual that the thing attains its concrete reality. Ultimate reality is in God, but phenomenal reality, finite reality, is in the individuality of separate things, and nowhere else.

The question inevitably arises, at many points in Nicholas's doctrine of God and the world,

[1] *De Trin.*, xv, 13. Cf. St. Thomas Aquinas, *Summa theol.*, I, q. 14, a. 8.

whether his system is pantheistic. He was certainly not a pantheist in intention, nor can he be made to appear such, unless we lay unfair stress upon paradoxical statements about God and the All. Philosophically, it ought to be sufficient to exempt his system from the charge of pantheism that Nicholas steadily maintains the difference between God and the world as the difference between unity and multiplicity, between infinitude and finitude, between necessity and contingency, between the absolute and the relative, between the Creator and the creation.[1] In the more technically theological sense, it is of vital importance that he maintains that the act of creation is strictly an act of the Divine Will.[2] It is difficult to see how, within the range of his own characteristic conceptions and terminology, he could safeguard essential theism more effectually than he does. All things are the world, and all things are God, but it is all things in their finite existence that constitute the world, and it is all things in their infinite essence that are in God. Actuality is in God, and in the world, and nowhere else; but God is pure actuality in Himself, and the world only attains actuality, and that a limited actuality, in individual things. God is unoriginated; the world has its origin from God. God is absolute being; the world is derived, dependent, relative being. In short, God is the Creator and the world is the creation. On the other hand, as has been already pointed out, the doctrine that the nature of God is absolutely

---

[1] Lenz, *Die docta ignorantia des Nikolaus Cusanus*, p. 52.
[2] *De beryllo*, xxiii, p. 275; *De ludo globi*, i, p. 213; *De genesi*, p. 131; *Excit.*, iii (*Verbum caro factum est*), p. 418.

undifferentiated, and that therefore what we conceive differently as His nature, His knowledge, His will, are all one and the same, undoubtedly makes the world seem more like an emanation from the essence of God than a product of His will. A tendency of this kind looks pantheistic in contrast to the opposite tendency of traditional orthodoxy, but it might be urged that orthodox doctrine has been always in quite as much danger of deism as Nicholas's teaching is in danger of pantheism.

Every doctrine of God must be poised between the two poles of Transcendence and Immanence. Every exaggeration of the transcendence of God moves in the direction of deism ; every exaggeration of the immanence of God moves in the direction of pantheism. In Nicholas's writings there are the most extreme expressions of both aspects of the truth, and the attempt to reconcile these results in profound inconsistencies which give a double sense to many terms like *explicatio*, *actualitas*, *coniectura*. Here explication means a separating tendency toward the finite ; there explication means a uniting tendency toward the infinite. Here actuality is found in God alone ; there actuality is found in individual existences alone. Here conjecture gives us truth, because it approaches the truth in increasing degrees, though it never gives us precise truth ; there conjecture does not give us truth, because it never gives us precise truth, though it approaches the truth in increasing degrees. It has been said that these inconsistencies in Nicholas's thought are due to the strife in his mind between the philosopher and the Christian.[1]

[1] Falckenberg, *Grundzüge*, p. 24.

Rather, they are due to the profound antinomies which beset all thought about the infinite, and which account for the paradoxes that are found, for example, in all the mystics. From what has preceded it will already be obvious to those who are familiar with the sources that Nicholas adopts from the pseudo-Dionysius and Erigena the whole method of the *theologia negativa*. The absolutely greatest is absolutely one, for it knows no distinction, and it has no opposite, and hence, strictly speaking, it is nameless. For all names arise from some singularity in the rational ground of things, by which one thing is distinguished from another. Where All is One, no particular name can be given. So Hermes Trismegistus [1] declares that God is the Allness of things (*universitas rerum*),[2] and hence He has no name, for either we must name God with every name, or we must name the All with His name, since in His unity the All of things is included. But the unity of God is not unity in the ordinary sense, which is opposed to plurality. The Oneness of God is such that it is opposed to no otherness, to no plurality, to no manifoldness. All, without composition or combination, is included in the pure identity of that

---

[1] The reference seems to be to *Poemandres*, v, 10 (Scott's *Hermetica*, i, p. 162). καὶ διὰ τοῦτο αὐτὸς ὀνόματα ἔχει ἅπαντα, ὅτι ἑνὸς αὐτοῦ πάντα ἐστὶ πατρός· καὶ διὰ τοῦτο αὐτὸς ὄνομα οὐκ ἔχει, ὅτι πάντων ἐστὶ πατήρ.

[2] The printed texts read : Quoniam Deus est universitas unum, tunc nullum nomen proprium est eius (*De doct. ign.*, i, 24, p. 18). Scharpff (*Des Cardinal Nicolaus von Cusa wichtigste Schriften*, p. 27) reads : *universitas rerum*. This agrees better with the line of argument, and also with the reference to Hermes Trismegistus.

Unity where there is nothing other, nothing diverse; where each and all are most truly present, not according to their own finitude, but as one in the surpassing unity of God. Whoever can name this nameless Unity which, while it is one, is yet all, has found the name of God.

Hence it is clear that the affirmative names of God can only apply to Him in an infinitely little degree (*per infinitum diminute*), for they only predicate of Him, though in a supreme sense, some attribute of the creature. Therefore all affirmative names are insufficiently inclusive. Our conceptions of truth, of virtue, of substance, for example, all depend for their significance upon their implicit opposition to our conceptions of falsehood, of vice, of accident. But there is no opposite to the conception of God. He is not what He is relatively to anything else, but absolutely. Affirmative names, when used of God, only apply to Him in relation to the created world. Not that the created thing is really the source of the name, or of the conception which is behind the name, for the created thing possesses nothing that is not from God. It is in relation to the creation, for example, that God is named the Creator, but God was able to create, and was therefore essentially the Creator, from all eternity, or He would not have possessed omnipotence. So that the name Creator, though it refers to the creation, is yet really prior to everything that is created. So with every other name of God: He is named the Father, the Son, the Holy Spirit, in His relation to the created world. It is in the created world that we learn the names and find the conceptions of fatherhood, and sonship,

and spirit.   But these, as we find them exemplified
in the human family and in the human soul, all
have their source in God—in the Unity, the Equality
and the Connexion, which constitute His triune
nature.[1] The negative theology is a necessary
complement of the positive theology, for without
it God could not be honoured as the infinite.
God is indefinable, because He is greater than all that
can be uttered or that can be thought.   All our
knowledge is by way of distinction and difference,
and since God is beyond all distinction and difference He is unknowable to the mind of man in
the essential mystery of His being.[2]   In this sense
we may even speak of the non-being of God, for
He does not exist in the same sense as anything
else that we know exists.[3]   The one thing we can
conceive of Him is that He is inconceivable.[4]   His
existence is superexistence.   This doctrine, which
Nicholas found fully developed in Dionysius,
Erigena, and Eckhart, (and more recklessly stated
than he himself ever states it) is fundamental to his

[1] *De doct. ign.*, i, 24, pp. 18–20.

[2] But the nature of God is known to us in Christ.   *Excit.*,
vi (*Debitores sumus*), p. 552.

[3] *Excit.*, vii (*Cum omni militia*), p. 556.   Generally Nicholas
is much more reluctant than Erigena and Eckhart to equate
Deus and *nihil*.   Probably the crucial passage in his writings
on this point is one in the dialogue *De Deo abscondito*, p.
338, which ends : Deus est supra nihil et aliquid : quia
ipsi obedit nihil, ut fiat aliquid.

[4] So constantly in Erigena and in Eckhart.   Deus, qui
per seipsum incomprehensibilis est.   *De div. nat.*, i, 11 (451,
B, vol. 122, ed. Migne).   See also i, 8 (447, C), i, 66 (510,
B, C).   Diu gotheit ist ein geistlich substancie, diu ungrunt-
lich ist, also daz nieman davon gesprechen kan, wie daz si.
Pfeiffer, *Meister Eckhart*, p. 524.   See also pp. 269 and 531.

whole scheme of thought.[1] According to the
negative theology, God is not Father, nor Son, nor
Spirit, but only Infinitude, and Infinitude as such
neither begets nor is begotten nor proceeds. But
Infinitude considered as Unity is the Father; considered as Equality is the Son; considered as Connexion is the Spirit.

The negations are true, and the affirmations are
true, but the negations are more true than the
affirmations. For the perfection of God is unspeak-
able and therefore cannot be defined, but we can
define imperfection, and deny it, and the more of
imperfection a negation removes from our idea of
the perfect Being, the truer it is.[2] When an artist
carves from a block of wood a statue of a king, he
cuts away all that is superfluous, all that hinders
the royal likeness from emerging, and that likeness
he has mentally before him all the time. And so,
when we represent God to ourselves, remembering
that He is better than all that can be represented,
we must cast away all thought of what is limited
and concrete—of corporeality, for God is spiritual;
of sense and imagination, for these can only func-
tion in a world of sense; of understanding and
reason, for these are also limited, and cannot
attain the final truth.[3] It is only by thus rejecting
every definite determination that we approach most
nearly to the absolute conception of God.

But we may know God by way of symbol and

---

[1] Hasse, *Nikolaus von Kues*, p. 79.

[2] *De doct. ign.*, i, 26, pp. 21, 22. Cf. Erigena, *De div. nat.*,
iii, 20 (684, D, vol. 122, ed. Migne).

[3] *De quaerendo Deum*, p. 298. Cf. Dionysius, *Mystical
Theology*, ii.

similitude. Visible things are images of the invisible world. Therefore, though God is beyond knowledge, He can be known in His works, as in a glass, darkly. The image is really an image ; it is really like the exemplar in some degree, but it might be more and more like it, in endless degrees of resemblance. Thus, while God is beyond the reach of our understanding, it is possible for us to know Him in a real, if only in a symbolic and approximate way. For the desire for God is implanted in the human soul, and it is not possible to desire or to love what is utterly unknown.[1] We can know God by symbols, therefore, and it is in mathematics that we find the most adequate symbols, because mathematics is the most fixed and the most certain (*firmissima atque certissima*) of the sciences.[2] But even mathematics, which mirrors the truth most fully and accurately, still only gives us symbols, though they are symbols of indestructible truth.[3]

Nicholas might have said, like Descartes, *omnia apud me mathematica fiunt*. He regarded mathematics as giving a kind of certitude that is not possible in other studies. This was not merely a mathematician's prejudice in favour of his own special study :[4] it depended upon a philosophical

---

[1] Nihil enim penitus incognitum appetitur. *Idiota*, i, p. 140. Cf. *Excit.*, v (*Suscepimus*), p. 503.

[2] *De doct. ign.*, i, 11, p. 8.

[3] *Compl. theol.*, i, p. 1107.

[4] Nicholas was one of the great mathematicians of his age. I have not the necessary knowledge to judge of his mathematical originality, or his importance in the development of the science. But the historians of mathematics speak of him with considerable respect. See Cantor, *Vorlesungen über die Geschichte der Mathematik*, ii, pp. 186, 211.

principle.   There is no precise equality in sensible
things : there can only be an approximate likeness.
No two things are exactly alike, and therefore there
is nothing which can serve as a precise measure of
anything else.   Since our knowledge of sensible
things is always by a more or less—by grouping
them into species and genera which are collections
of things more or less alike, but never exactly
alike—our knowledge of these things is itself a
more or less, an approximation to the truth, but
never the exact truth and never the whole truth.
But with the abstractions of mathematics it is otherwise.   The ideal numbers and ideal quantities
and ideal figures of the mathematician can be
exactly alike, because they are ideal, and so precise
and final truth is possible in mathematical symbols.

Nicholas points out that many mathematical
examples have been used, in the very highest ranges
of theological thought, by writers in the past.
Anselm compared the highest truth with an infinite
line,[1] and others, seeking to set forth the highest
actuality, or the highest unity, have likened God
to an infinite sphere or an infinite circle, while still
others have likened the Trinity to a triangle which
has three equal sides and three equal angles.   All
are right, and all have essentially the same thought,
for the infinite line, the infinite triangle, the infinite
circle, and the infinite sphere, are all one and the
same.   This may be proved in the following way.
The infinite line is straight.   Now the circumference of a circle is a curved line, and the greater
the circle is, the less is the curve of its circumference, so that the circumference of the greatest

[1] *De veritate*, X, xiii (478, D ; 486, B, vol. 158, ed. Migne).

possible circle is not curved at all, but straight.
Therefore the infinite circle coincides with the infinite straight line.   If one end of a line is taken as a
pivot, and the line is moved around some distance,
it describes a triangle.   If it is moved around to its
starting-point, it describes a circle.   If it is moved
around to its opposite point, it describes a semicircle, and if this semicircle is moved around its
unmoved diameter, it describes a sphere.   Now
the infinite line is in actuality all that the finite
line is in possibility ; therefore the infinite line
is an infinite triangle, an infinite circle, and an
infinite sphere.[1]

[1] *De doct. ign.*, i, 13, 14, 15, pp. 9–11.

CHAPTER II

THE COINCIDENCE OF CONTRARIES

NICHOLAS continually expressed the ultimate identification of God and the world in geometrical and mathematical terms. The most important of all such are the terms maximum and minimum, which recur perpetually. A large part of Nicholas's system depends upon his use of the doctrine that God is the absolute maximum and also the absolute minimum, which coincide. The greatest is that than which there can be nothing greater, and the highest fullness (*abundantia*) is always Oneness, for Oneness is Being (*entitas*). Hence the greatest being is the greatest unity, and the greatest unity is absolutely free from all relation and all concreteness (*contractione*), and manifestly has no opposite. The absolute maximum is therefore a unity that is all and in all, since it is the maximum. Because it has no opposite, it coincides with the minimum.[1]

Everything finite and limited comes from the one absolute maximum, and that maximum is necessary, as the beginning and end of the finite. Nothing could be if that were not. The maximum has no opposite either in concrete being or in non-being. It exists as absolute necessity. It cannot be other than it is. It cannot be greater

[1] *De doct. ign.*, i, 2, p. 2.

than it is, since it is the maximum; it cannot be less than it is, or it would not be the maximum, and because it cannot be less than it is, it coincides with the minimum. And the minimum cannot be less than it is, since it is the minimum; neither can it be greater than it is, or it would not be the minimum, and because it cannot be greater than it is, it coincides with the maximum.

God, thus conceived as the coincidence of the maximum and the minimum, and as the coincidence of all contraries, is the essence of all; all things are what they are, or were, or will be, actually and eternally only in Him.[1] Since God is pure being, which is one, eternal, infinite, changeless, it follows that things are in God in so far as they possess unity and eternity, infinity and immutability, but in so far as they are multiple and mutable, local and temporal, they are unreal, and not in God. Yet it is God, as the innermost principle of reality, Who sustains all the world of phenomena, so that unity becomes the principle of multiplicity, and eternity of time, and so with the rest. This relation between God and the world is illustrated by the relation between the infinite line and the finite line. The finite line is divisible, the infinite is

---

[1] *De doct. ign.*, i, 6, p. 12. Nicholas expressly refers this type of doctrine to Eckhart, in one of his sermons. Deus non est nisi in esse: tunc (dicit magister Eccardus) non est in tempore, nec divisione, nec continuo seu quantitate, nec in aliquo habente magis et minus, nec in distincto, nec in ullo creato ut est hoc vel illud, nec in ullo proprio: licet sit in omnibus ut sunt entia. *Excit.*, vii (*Ubi est qui natus est rex Iudaeorum*), p. 570. There are many passages in Eckhart which might be quoted in illustration. See Pfeiffer, *Meister Eckhart*, pp. 95, 133, 177, 222, 531.

not, but the finite line is not divisible into a non-line, so that the finite line is indivisible as to its essence, for a line one foot long is as much a line as a line two feet long. Hence the infinite line is the rational ground (*ratio*) of the finite line. So also the maximum is the rational ground of all, and as such the measure of all. If there are two lines, one of two feet and the other of three feet, the essence of the line is alike in each : the difference consists in the length. In the infinite line this difference falls away and only the rational ground of the line remains. The difference between two lines does not lie in the rational ground which both possess but in the fact that they do not participate in an equally perfect way in the rational ground. The infinite line is wholly in each line so that each line is in it, and these two relations are to be understood together. The maximum is in each thing and in nothing, for the maximum is in each thing in the same relation in which each thing is in it, and it is itself this relation.[1]

The curved line, which may be a more or a less, cannot be the maximum line, for it is, as a *curved* line, nothing, because the curve is a decline from the straight. But the *being* of the curved line also is a participation in the straight line, for the absolutely greatest or absolutely least curve is the straight line. Now things participate in being, as the curve in the straight. The straight finite line participates simply and immediately in the infinite line, but the curved line participates mediately through the straight finite line in the infinite line ; so it is also with all things, whence results the

[1] *De doct. ign.*, i, 17, pp. 12–13.

difference between substance and accident. The
most adequate measure for both is the maximum,
which is neither substance nor accident, though it is
nearer substance than accident, and therefore is
called the more-than-substance, or supersubstantial.[1] That is to say, substance has a more direct
participation in ultimate being than accident, for
accident has its derived and dependent being from
substance, whereas substance has its being from the
supersubstantial. If the supersubstantial is represented by the infinite straight line, the things in the
world that are more real are like finite straight
lines, which really resemble, in a limited way, the
infinite straight line, but the things in the world
that are less real are like curved lines, which derive
all the being they possess from participation in
the infinite straight line, through the finite straight
line, but which are less and less real as the curve
increases—as they fall away more and more from
the rectitude of infinite reality.

The conception of the maximum, as applied to
God, is undoubtedly derived from Anselm,[2] a
great deal of whose thought revolved around it.
It is, of course, the core of Anselm's famous ontological argument. We meet the thought almost at
the beginning of the *Proslogion* : 'We believe that
Thou art somewhat than which no greater can be
conceived' (*aliquid, quo nihil maius cogitari possit*),[3]

[1] *De doct. ign.*, i, 18, pp. 13–14. Compare the language of
Eckhart : Spriche ich ouch : got ist ein wesen, ez ist niht
war ; er ist ein überswebende wesen und ein überwesende
nihtheit. Pfeiffer, *Meister Eckhart*, p. 319.

[2] Fiorentino, *Rinascimento filosofico nel quattrocento*, pp.
113–14.

[3] *Proslogion*, ii (227, D, vol. 158, ed. Migne).

and it recurs continually in Anselm's writings. In one direction Nicholas develops Anselm's argument rather curiously. The existence of God is necessary, not merely, as with Anselm, because existence is one of the attributes which is involved in the very conception of perfection, but because only four hypotheses regarding the existence of God are possible, and whichever we adopt, we have finally to admit the fact. Either God exists; or He does not exist; or He both-exists-and-does-not-exist; or He neither-exists-nor-does-not-exist.[1] Now whichever hypothesis we adopt, we necessarily regard as the greatest truth, and that means that we admit, in spite of ourselves, a maximum—a maximum in the highest range of thought, a maximum of truth, which is the same as the absolute maximum, for there is only one simplex maximum in reality, and every maximum that we can separately conceive is merely a subjective aspect of it. Thus there is no truth which is so certainly true as the existence of God, because God is the absolute truth, and as the absolute truth, the necessary truth; it is impossible that He should not exist. The only sense in which we can speak of the non-being of God is the philosophical and mystical sense: as we oppose time and eternity because time is measurable and eternity is immeasurable, so we may oppose existence and non-existence, because the one is limited and the other is unlimited, and in this sense we may say that God does not exist. But in any other sense it is strictly

[1] *De doct. ign.*, i, 6, p. 5; *De coniecturis*, i, 7, p. 80. See also *Excit.*, vii (*Cum omnia militia*), p. 556.

This is derived from Augustine, *De lib. arbitr.*, ii, 14, 15.

unthinkable that God should not exist. If He exists, that is the truth; if He does not exist, that is the truth. If it were possible for both these propositions to be true at the same time, that would be the truth. If it were possible for both to be false at the same time, that would be the truth. In any case the truth exists, and the maximum of truth. In any case there is an absolute and necessary existence of the truth, and of the truth in its highest and most general range, a *maximum veritatis*. And that absolute, necessary, universal existence of the truth *is* the existence of God. Generally, however, Nicholas does not use the conception of the maximum with reference to necessary existence, but merely as the equivalent of what we should call the absolute,[1] and as the equivalent of the minimum, in his doctrine of the coincidence of contraries.

This principle of the coincidence of contraries Nicholas himself regarded as the central truth of his system.[2] He tells us that it flashed upon his

[1] Rossi, *Niccolò di Cusa e la Direzione Monistica della Filosofia nel Rinascimento*, pp. 45–6, justly points out that there is a marked difference in the way the conception is used in Anselm and in Nicholas. But this does not affect the undoubted fact that Nicholas borrowed the notion of the maximum from Anselm in the first place.

[2] There can be no doubt that Nicholas's doctrine of the coincidence of contraries derives largely from Eckhart, who consistently regards all oppositions as coalescing into unity in the simplicity of real being. Thus for example, he writes: Waz ist widersatzunge? Lieb unde leit, wiz unde swarz, daz hat widersatzunge unde diu enblibet in wesenne niht. . . . Swenne diu seele kumt in daz lieht der vernünftekeit, so weiz si niht widersatzunge. Pfeiffer, *Meister Eckhart*, p. 264.

mind during his voyage from Constantinople (i.e. about December 1437, or January 1438), and he writes of it as if it were almost a supernatural revelation.[1] He supports this doctrine with a wealth of subtle illustrations and acute arguments of which the most important are these. The maximum is the greatest possible greatness, the minimum is the greatest possible littleness. We are then bidden to think away quantity as irrelevant, and we are left with merely the notion of a greatest possible, in which the maximum and minimum coincide. It does not seem to have occurred to Nicholas, in advancing this naïve argument, that it is precisely quantity with which (according to his own definition) the maximum and minimum are concerned, and that if you think away quantity the terms become simply meaningless. It is like saying that black and red are really the same, because if you think away colour, the terms coincide. They do, in the sense of being emptied of all meaning. It may be urged that this is unfair to our philosopher because what was really in his mind was that when the notion of quantity is abstracted from the maximum and the minimum there does remain the indefinite thought of an utmost possible. But even so that thought is turned one way in the idea of a maximum, and the other way in the idea of a minimum. To say that these last coincide on the strength of that residual thought is like saying that a road which goes east is the same as a road which goes south,

---

[1] In mari ex Graecia rediens, credo superno dono a patre luminum, a quo omne datum optimum, ad hoc ductus sum. *De doct. ign.*, iii, 12 (*epil.*), p. 62. Cf. *De vis. Dei*, p. 189.

because if you think away east and south you are left with only the general notion of undefined direction, in which both roads coincide.

Again Nicholas argues that the maximum and the minimum coincide because the maximum cannot be less, and is therefore a minimum, and because the minimum cannot be more, and is therefore a maximum. But this, again, is surely the merest equivocation. The maximum cannot be less than it is, *to be the greatest*; the minimum cannot be more than it is, *to be the least*.[1] But the whole meaning of the terms lies there in the condition which he suppresses—that the minimum is so small that it cannot be less, and if it were greater it would not be the least; and the maximum is so great that it cannot be more, and if it were less it would not be the greatest; and when once that essential condition is expressed the terms cannot be interchanged. When you express the character of the minimum by saying that it is so little that it cannot be less, you cannot apply that phrase to the maximum, and when you express the character of the maximum by saying that it is so great that it cannot be greater, you cannot apply that phrase to the minimum. That is to say, the maximum and the minimum do not coincide, and cannot be made to appear to do so when they are adequately described; it is only on the strength of a defective definition, which omits the most essential characteristic of each, that their coincidence can be made to appear possible.

Nicholas also teaches that the maximum and the minimum coincide in God, because nothing can

[1] Stöckl, *Geschichte der Philosophie des Mittelalters*, iii, p. 82.

be conceived greater or smaller than God, since He is not of the same nature as things which admit of a more and less. This again seems particularly futile, for the whole significance of the terms maximum and minimum, when applied otherwise than to God, consists in their use as the terminals of a series of more and less. When Nicholas uses the words maximum and minimum in relation to things in the universe, he uses them in this sense, as the final terms of an ascending scale of greatness and a descending scale of smallness; when he uses them of God he uses them merely to suggest that those scales cannot apply to the Divine Nature. In the one case the words express a definite, positive and quantitative content; in the other case they merely suggest that any such content is unthinkable. On the one hand, they are used to express the extremes of comparison; on the other, they merely say that no comparison is possible.

And yet, while the doctrine of Nicholas is fairly open to criticism of this sort, and while much of it really seems to be subtle and skilful equivocation, one does feel that there is more than that in his central idea of the coincidence of contraries, and in his passion for unity.[1] The fact is that Nicholas was obsessed by that thought of the Absolute which has been the preoccupation of all idealistic philosophy since Kant. The world was to him the

[1] Rossi, *Niccolò di Cusa e la Direzione Monistica della Filosofia nel Rinascimento*, p. 69; Ranft, *Schöpfer und Geschöpf nach Kardinal Nikolaus von Cusa*, p. 66; Glossner, *Nikolaus von Cusa und Marius Nizolius als Vorläufer der neueren Philosophie*, p. 21.

realm of the comparative, the relative, and he was always dominated by the thought of the superlative and the absolute which all the graded existence of the world implied and necessitated. His problem, in fact, though he naturally treated it according to the conceptions and in the terms of his own day, was precisely that of Mr. F. H. Bradley.

It is a universe of contrasts, contradictions, antitheses, anomalies, and there must be some secret of ultimate reconciliation. There must be a region where oppositions blend into each other, where contradictions merge into the larger truth, where all is concordant and consistent, because all coalesces into a final unity. Nicholas identified this Absolute with God, as every religious thinker must. God is absolute Truth, absolute Goodness, absolute Being, and all that is many and diverse in the universe is one and the same in His absolute unity and His absolute identity.[1] The whole doctrine of the coincidence of contraries is, in fact, an elaboration of the essential principle of the *theologia negativa*.[2] The superexistence of God can only be expressed by negations, because it surpasses all our positive conceptions, and in it all the contradictions of finite existence fall away into ineffable unity.

It was the antinomies of the world that always preoccupied Nicholas, as indeed they always preoccupy the philosophic mind. Especially it was the difficulties that arise out of the relation between the infinite Creator and the finite creation. How can multiple, imperfect, limited existence derive from the One, the Perfect, the Infinite? How is the contingent related to the necessary, the tem-

[1] *De vis. Dei*, p. 193.   [2] *Apologia*, p. 64.

poral to the eternal, the particular to the universal ?
The answer is given by way of the correlative
notions of *complicatio* and *explicatio*. There is only
one maximum, the greatest of all greatests, which
has no opposite, and therefore coincides with the
minimum. Every perfection is included in the
perfection of God : if there were any perfection
that were not, then it would be possible for the
perfection of God to be yet more perfect, and it
would not be infinite perfection.[1] Everything,
in its perfection, is therefore included in the absolute maximum, and the infinite unity is the aggregate
(*complicatio*) of all. So too, identity is the complication of difference, and likeness of unlikeness.
God is therefore the complication or aggregate of
all, in the sense that all is in Him. He is the explication or development of all so far as He is in all.[2]
God is thus the aggregate (*complicatio*) of all things,
as the essential and eternal ground of their being.
Things are the evolution (*explicatio*) of God, as the
finite, multiple, differentiated development of what
is grounded in Him, though in Him the finite is
infinitude, the multiple is unity, and the difference
is identity.[3] There is, so to speak, one ultimate

[1] *Apologia*, p. 72.

[2] Deus ergo est omnia complicans, in hoc quod omnia
in eo, est omnia explicans, in hoc quia ipse in omnibus.
De doct. ign., ii, 3, p. 26.

[3] So constantly in Eckhart : Niht enhindert die sele so
sere an der bekentnisse gotes als zit unde stat. Zit unde
stat sint stücke unde got ist ein. Darumbe, sol diu sele
got erkennen, so muoz si in erkennen oben zit und oben
stat ; want got enist weder diz noch daz, als disiu manic-
valtiu dinc : want got ist ein. Pfeiffer, *Meister Eckhart*,
p. 222. See also pp. 5 and 39.

being, which may be viewed from two sides.[1]
On the higher side, it is One and Absolute, super-
existent, the essence of all that is—God. On the
lower side, it is multiple and relative, a derived and
dependent existence, an evolution into the visible
and the temporal—the universe.

Nicholas more than once uses the term evolution [2] as equivalent to explication, which is his more
usual phrase. Since all begins from the superessential unity, the perfect precedes the imperfect,[3]
the immutable precedes the changeable, the eternal
precedes the temporal. The act of creation is
therefore essentially a limitation of the unlimited,
the evolution of the finite which was eternally
involved in the infinite. Obviously it is only in
some such sense that a religious philosophy can
speak of evolution at all. Religion must regard
God as the source of all that is, and therefore
must hold that all that becomes explicit in the
universe (to borrow Nicholas's style) is first implicit
in God, at least as lying within that sphere of
possibility which is constituted by His nature and
His will.

But the term explication does not carry a constant significance in Nicholas's writings. The
whole span of existence is conceived as a circle,
which begins and ends in God. There is a down-
ward curve representing the passage of the infinite
into the finite, and there is an upward curve representing the passage of the finite into the infinite.

[1] Eucken, *Nicolaus von Cues*, in *Philosophische Monatshefte*,
xiv, (1878), pp. 450–1.
[2] Evolutio, id est, explicatio. *De mente*, ix, p. 162.
[3] *De doct. ign.*, ii, 3, p. 26.

Or, to vary the metaphor, there is a centrifugal movement, from God to the world, and a centripetal movement, from the world to God. One is the departure from Unity into the multiple, the different, the separate; the other is the return of all the multiplicity and difference and separateness of the world into Unity. Now Nicholas uses the term explication of *both* these movements. One is manifestly a limitation, an impoverishment, a descent; the other is manifestly an expansion, an enrichment, an ascent; and yet *explicatio* stands for both. This is not merely a matter of occasional laxity in the use of a phrase; it is the steady employment of a term in altogether inconsistent senses. It is utterly impossible to regard an analytic, individualizing, materializing movement in the direction of the finite as being really of the same kind as a synthetic, generalizing, spiritualizing movement in the direction of the infinite.[1]

A similar inconsistency infects Nicholas's doctrine of actuality. Absolute actuality is in God alone; concrete actuality is only in the individual existence. Yet the reality of things is in human knowledge more truly than in the things themselves, for they exist in knowledge in a higher mode than in their individual reality, because knowledge, as a unifying principle, approaches nearer to the unity of God. And the aggregate of all concrete reality is in the Logos. In one direction, therefore, things are more actual as they approach the pure actuality of God and are nearer to the very source of concrete actuality in the Logos. In another

[1] J. R. Charbonnel, *La Pensée Italienne au XVIe Siècle*, pp. 466–7.

direction things are more actual the more individual and the more separate they are. It is true that Nicholas avoids a formal contradiction by steadily distinguishing between the absolute actuality and the concrete actuality, but if any real meaning attaches to actuality it is difficult to see how one can approach it, however it may be qualified, by going further in one direction and also by going further in the opposite direction. His doctrine amounts to this : the more abstract, simplex, united, the more actual ; and also the more concrete, complex, separate, the more actual.[1]

This kind of ambiguity penetrates Nicholas's thought, as well as his terminology, and is evident in many places. Thus he teaches that though there are no real differences in the absolute simplicity of the nature of God, yet God is the absolute reason, and comprises in Himself all rational distinctions,[2] and is therefore the aggregate of all that exists, and even of the contradictions which inhere in all that exists.[3] Elsewhere he says that while the universe has from God its unity, discreteness, and connexion, yet in so far as its unity is in plurality, its discreteness in confusion, its connexion in discord, it is not from God, and has no positive cause.[4] But if what is rational is real (and there is nothing Nicholas holds more strongly), how

---

[1] Cf. Falckenberg, *Grundzüge*, pp. 54-5.

[2] *De vis. Dei*, iii, p. 182 ; *Excit.*, ix (*Ecce ascendimus*), p. 646 ; *De vis. Dei*, vii, p. 186.

[3] Deum esse omnium complicationem, etiam contradictoriorum. *De doct. ign.*, i, 22, p. 17. Cf. *De ludo globi*, ii, p. 229.

[4] *De doct. ign.*, ii, 2, p. 24.

can there be rational distinctions in the Godhead which are not real distinctions?

The fact is that there is implicit in Nicholas's metaphysics, thoroughgoing as he intends his monism to be, a kind of Manichaean dualism. He says again and again, with a reminiscence of Plato, that God is free from envy, and therefore cannot communicate a lessened being; God seeks to impart Himself to all that exists, and He is in all things in the universe as far as the nature of each thing will allow.[1] But the nature of things will only allow the infinite reality to be present in various finite degrees, and therefore a lessened being is communicated from God. All created existence is a declension from infinitude, a lapse into the imperfect. But why must it be so? Nicholas does not consistently say, like St. Thomas Aquinas, that it is the will of God that the limitations and divisions and oppositions of the universe should exist, and that it is not possible for the human mind to go behind the will of God. He says that God cannot communicate Himself to the universe otherwise than He does, because the nature of the universe will not allow any more than this partial and distorted image of the One and the Eternal to be manifested in it, precisely as a series of curved mirrors can only reflect partial and distorted images of what is placed before them.[2]

Surely this means that the omnipotence of God

---

[1] *De doct. ign.*, ii, 2, p. 24. So constantly in Eckhart; See Pfeiffer, *Meister Eckhart*, pp. 272 and 479; Jostes, *Meister Eckhart und seine Jünger*, p. 1; Lasson, *Meister Eckhart, der Mystiker*, p. 128.

[2] *De fil. Dei*, p. 122.

is limited by a defect which inheres in the finite, and, for all practical purposes, in the material. It is one thing to say that the universe is as it is because the finiteness of the finite is a determination of the will of God, like everything else that exists (and there are passages where Nicholas does practically say this, which illustrates the contradictory character of his postulates). It is quite another thing to say, as he generally does say, in effect, that the finiteness of the finite is a kind of natural and necessary obstacle which prevents God from manifesting Himself perfectly in the universe, as it is the essential impulse of His nature to do.

It is at this point that Nicholas uses the notion of *contractio* [1] to explain the nature of the finite universe. All things in the world derive from God, and not merely so, but all things share, as far as it is possible for them to share, the likeness of God. [2] From God, as the first and absolute Unity, issues a second unity, the universe, which is the unity of creation. In the order of nature, though not in that of time, the universal precedes the particular; and the universe holds together in a relative unity all that exists, except the absolute existence of God. Then from this second unity issues a third unity, that of the genera, and from this a fourth unity, that of the species. The universe is constituted by the genera, the genera are constituted by the species, the species are constituted by the individuals. It is only in this descending

---

[1] Duex, *Der deutsche Cardinal Nicolaus von Cusa*, ii, p. 322.
[2] This is Eckhart's doctrine. Aber got der giuzet sich doch weselich in alle creaturen, in iegliche als vil si enpfahen mac. Pfeiffer, *Meister Eckhart*, p. 273.

series that ultimate being can realize itself in concrete existence, which implies and involves difference and multiplicity. Each lower stage represents the absolute Unity as far as its restricted nature allows. Thus in the order of nature there is a passage from the absolute Unity of God to multiplicity, through three relative unities, each of which exists only as an idea, actualized in the last resort by the existence of the individual.

It is not merely the unity of God which is thus reflected in the world: the triune nature of the Deity is reflected also.[1] In all concrete existence there is necessarily that which is contractable (*contrahibile*), that which contracts (*contrahens*), and that which unites the two (*nexus*). The first is possibility, the second is necessity, and they are related as matter and form. (It is, in Nicholas's terms, concrete possibility and concrete necessity that are meant, for God is absolute possibility and absolute necessity.) Then, third, there is the principle of union—that which unites the possible and the necessary into the actual. So that in all things there is this threefoldness, of concrete possibility, concrete necessity, and concrete union, or of *potentia*, *actus*, *nexus*.[2]

It follows directly from this that there is a strong emphasis in Nicholas's philosophy upon individual existence, upon the actuality of the particular, and

---

[1] So repeatedly in the writings of Eckhart: Die drie personen hant geworht ir eigen bilde an allen creaturen, die redelich sint. Pfeiffer, *Meister Eckhart*, p. 503. See also p. 408.

[2] Coaeterna ergo sunt absoluta potentia, et actus, et utriusque nexus. *De Possest*, p. 250.

this in two directions. The individuality of the individual is strongly stressed. There are no two things in the world precisely alike. Precise equality is identity, and is only found in the nature of God. If it could be found as between two things in the world it would mean that they were not two things but one. Every existing thing, therefore, possesses a unique individuality and a unique actuality. And, on the other hand, the universality of the particular is strongly emphasized, in a way that reminds one of Leibniz, and that may perhaps have had some remote influence upon Leibnizian doctrine. Every particular thing in the world is a reflection and a recapitulation of the universe, a literal microcosm. The universe, the second unity, like God, the first unity, is in everything as far as the nature of the thing will allow. And everything in the world is in everything else, as far as the nature of the thing will allow—*quodlibet in quolibet*, which is Nicholas's extension of the doctrine of ὁμοιομερεία that he found in Anaxagoras. An individual thing could not exist merely in itself; it only exists as a constituent part of the universe, and as it helps to make the whole, the whole helps to make it.[1] So that each individual thing is a contraction of the universe; the whole is mirrored in every fractional part. It may be remarked that this is defensible enough in the light of modern knowledge, for every fact, every force, every law, in the universe is operative throughout the universe, as far as the nature of separate things will permit. The laws of motion, for example, which govern the movements of the

[1] Ritter, *Die christliche Philosophie*, ii, pp. 11–12.

stars govern also the movement of particles of dust, so far as they are not annulled by the operation of other laws and other conditions : light penetrates everything in the universe equally, as far as the position and the structure of the thing will allow the penetration ; and so forth. In other words, every single fact in the universe has a universal quality, and conditions every other fact to the full extent that the constitution of that fact renders possible. It was this, which seems to be a structural principle of the universe, which was in the mind of Nicholas, and he gave it much more than a merely physical significance. It is here, at the point where he emphasizes the unique individuality, and at the same time the universal quality, which are possessed by every single thing in the universe, that he approaches most nearly, perhaps, to Plato. For while things are alike, yet no two things are exactly alike. There is, so to speak, a universal quality of likeness, and a particular characteristic of unlikeness, in everything that exists. This means that whatever degree of precision a thing possesses, it possesses because it is more or less a participant in, and more or less a likeness of, the absolute precision.[1] And so of all else : whatever of goodness or of truth, for example, a thing has, it has because to that extent it resembles and shares in the absolute goodness or the absolute truth.[2] But things in this world might always be more precise, or more true, or more good, because they might participate more and

---

[1] Here *participatio* and *imago* are evidently Plato's μέθεξις and μίμημα.

[2] *Idiota*, ii, p. 145.

more, to an endless extent, in the absolute qualities of precision, or of truth, or of goodness, and so on.

Here is Nicholas's doctrine of ideas, which may be perhaps called Platonic, in a way ; but it is Platonism with a difference. The issue between the Platonists and the Aristotelians is discussed in many places in Nicholas's writings.

The truth of the matter, Nicholas declares, is that there is no absolute form, or absolute possibility, or absolute actuality, except God. He is the Form of all forms.[1] The ideas of things are not separate, except as they exist in things in the world of space and time ; as absolute, they are undifferentiated. The forms of things are one in God, and that Form is God. All diversity is identity in God. The one universal Form comprehends all forms as one, but they only exist separately when they exist in things.[2]

Perhaps the most significant statement in the whole of Nicholas's writings upon this issue is a passage where he says expressly that there is not any medium between the absolute and the concrete,[3] as those ancient philosophers imagined who held that there was a world-soul existing as a distinct entity between God and the world. If

[1] *De mente*, ii, p. 151 ; *De ludo globi*, ii, pp. 260–1.

[2] *De doct. ign.*, ii, 9, pp. 34–6. The whole of this treatment of the forms of things and their relation to God is manifestly based upon a long discussion in one of Eckhart's sermons, *In omnibus requiem quaesivi*.

The whole discussion in Eckhart is confessedly based upon St. Thomas Aquinas, though no reference is given. It is evidently the *Summa theol.*, I, q. 15, a. 1–3, that Eckhart has in mind. Much of it is translated word for word.

[3] *De doct. ign.*, ii, 9, p. 36.

we are to speak of a world-soul, the world-soul is God; if we are to speak of the creative ideas, the creative ideas are the Logos, which is one with God. The whole notion of intermediaries between the unity of the Creator and the multiplicity of the world is thus definitely given up. The Neoplatonist conception which Nicholas inherited, and which was his point of departure, consistently thought of God and the world, first of all, as immeasurably apart, and then as linked together by creative principles which proceeded from God and then actualized the world. Nicholas thinks of God and the world as in the most intimate and the most necessary relation : the infinite and the finite are like two correlative aspects—the internal and the external, or the essential and the accidental, as we might say—in which all that is and all that can be exists. God is the one, eternal, uncreated, unchangeable essence of all that appears as multiple and mutable in the created universe.

The question of universals, which fills so large a place in the history of philosophic thought in the Middle Ages, and which is so closely connected with the doctrine of ideas, is dealt with by Nicholas on similar lines. The Peripatetics, he declares, are right in saying that universals have no actuality apart from things (*extra res*), for it is only individual existence, in which the universal has become concrete, that has actuality. The universal has a kind of potential being that is capable of becoming individual (*contrahibile per singulare*) : it is not anything, before concrete existence, other than a universal which is capable of concrete existence, not subsisting in itself, but in that which has actuality. Yet the universals are not mere notions (*solum entia rationis*), for they exist in things ; as the line is not a mere notion, though it does not exist outside of bodies, for it does exist in bodies. The rational abstraction, taken by itself, is indeed a mere notion, for it has not attained absolute being. The wholly absolute Universal is God (*Universale enim penitus absolutum Deus est*). But the universal exists in our minds as intellectually concrete. And thought is a higher kind of existence than the material existence of things. So that the universals really exist in our minds in a higher fashion than they exist in things.

CHAPTER III

THE TRINITY, AND THE PROBLEM OF EVIL

WHILE God is one, and the universe is one, and God, as Unity, is the one absolute Form and the one absolute Universal, the doctrine of the Trinity is fundamental in the whole of Nicholas's thought about God and equally about the world. And the triune nature of God is not merely a mysterious truth of revealed religion, but a philosophical necessity. For Unity involves Equality, and Unity and Equality involve Connexion.[1] Unity must be, so to speak, equal within itself, and connected within itself. Even from the external point of view, all otherness (*alteritas*) must involve oneness (*unitas*). And alterity is the same as inequality, and all inequality must involve equality. And alterity or inequality is the same as separation, and all separation must

---

[1] The whole conception, and the express terms, are from Augustine. In Patre unitas, in Filio aequalitas, in Spiritu Sancto unitatis aequalitatisque concordia. Et haec tria unum omnia propter Patrem, aequalia omnia propter Filium, connexa omnia propter Spiritum Sanctum. *De doctrina christiana*, i, 5. (We know that Nicholas read this book, because he quotes it in the *De concordantia catholica*.) The above passage is often quoted by medieval writers, e.g. Pope Leo III, *Epistola XVI*; Hugh of St. Victor, *Quaestiones in Epistolas Pauli*, Q. 283.

involve connexion. Unity, equality, and connexion must be eternal, for they must necessarily
precede alterity, inequality, and separation.[1] But
there cannot be more than one eternal maximum,[2]
therefore unity, equality, and connexion are eternally one. The generation of unity from unity is
a repetition of unity, or equality. The procession
from both is a repetition of the repetition of unity,
or connexion, for it is the uniting (*unitio*) of unity
and equality of unity. For procession is like an
extension from the one to the other. When two
things are alike the likeness extends or proceeds
from one to the other, conjoining and connecting
them.[3] Unity is being (*unitas dicitur quasi onitas,
ab ὄν graeco vocabulo, quod latine ens dicitur, et est unitas
entitas*). Equality of unity is thus equality of being.
Generation is repetition of unity.[4] Unity generates
unity, and this generation is eternal.[5] As equality
of unity is begotten of unity, and as connexion
proceeds from them both, so unity, equality of unity,
and connexion of equality and unity are one and the
same. Thus in humanity natural love unites the
one and the other, because of the likeness of nature
that exists between a father and a son. So the

[1] *De doct. ign.*, i, 7, p. 5.
[2] *De mente*, ii, p. 149.
[3] *De doct. ign.*, i, 9, p. 6.
[4] Once the Trinity is represented as a threefold repetition of equality. Est igitur aequalitas de se generans verbum, quod est eius aequalitas, a quibus procedit nexus, qui
est aequalitas ; quam nexum spiritum charitatis dicimus.
Quoniam ex aequalitate generante, et aequalitate genita, non
potest procedere, nisi aequalitas. *Excit.*, i (*Vita erit lux
hominum*), p. 371.
[5] *De doct. ign.*, i, 8, p. 6.

Father is Unity, the Son is Equality, and the Spirit is the Love which is the eternal connexion between the Father and the Son.[1]

The Trinity, so conceived, is then seen in many other triune aspects, as the loving Love, the love-worthy Love, and the uniting act of Love; [2] as that which knows, that which is known, and the uniting act of knowledge; [3] as possibility, actuality, and the motion which makes these one; [4] and is seen reflected in human experience, as spirit, soul, and body; [5] as memory, reason, and will; [6] and as the three theological virtues of faith, hope, and love; [7] and reflected again in the relation between God, angels, and men, in the Church triumphant, and in the relation between the sacraments, the priesthood, and the people, in the Church mili-

---

[1] De doct. ign., i, 9, pp. 6–7.

[2] Tu igitur, Deus meus, qui es amor, es amor amans, et amor amabilis, et amor, amoris amantis et amabilis nexus. De vis. Dei, xvii, p. 197. The thought is borrowed from Augustine. Amor autem alicuius amantis est, et amore aliquid amatur. Ecce tria sunt, amans, et quod amatur, et amor. De Trin., viii, 10, 14. Compare another of Nicholas's triads. In divina natura est foecunditas, proles, et amor. Foecunditas Deus est, qui et origo et Pater: proles autem ipsius foecunditatis, Filius: amor, nexus utriusque. De crib. Alch., ii, 5, p. 901.

[3] Intelligens, intelligibile, intelligere. De doct. ign., i, 10, p. 7.

[4] Scimus nunc ex istis universum trinum; et nihil universorum esse, quod non sit unum ex potentia, actu, et connexionis motu. De doct. ign., ii, 11, p. 37.

[5] De concord. cath., i, 6, p. 700.

[6] Memoria, intellectus, et voluntas. Excit., ii (Fides autem Catholica haec est), p. 385; Excit., iv (Ex ipso et per ipsum), p. 444.

[7] Excit., v (Benedicta sit), p. 468.

tant;[1] and in many mundane triads,[2] as centre, diameter, and circumference;[3] as beginning, middle, and end;[4] as the spring, the river, and the lake;[5] and so forth.

Like Erigena, Nicholas makes the Trinity the creative *schema* of the universe, but he works out the doctrine rather differently. In the Scot, Father, Son, and Spirit are consistently identified with the οὐσία, δύναμις, ἐνέργεια, *essentia*, *virtus*, *operatio*, which are present in all things. Several times Nicholas uses precisely this phrase,[6] and once he

[1] *De concord. cath.*, i, 6, p. 700. Cf. *De auctoritate praesidendi* (in Duex, i, p. 477).

[2] Sunt in unaquaque re trinitatis vestigia. *De doct. ign.*, i, 24, p. 20.

[3] *De doct. ign.*, i, 21, p. 16. Cf. Erigena, *De div. nat.*, i, 11 (451, D, vol. 122, ed. Migne).

[4] *De doct. ign.*, i, 21, p. 16; *De genesi*, p. 128; *Apologia*, p. 66.

[5] Fons unitas, fluvius aequalitas, nexus utriusque stagnum. *De crib. Alch.*, ii, p. 902. Cf. *Excit.*, vi (*Cum venerit Paracletus*), p. 530.

[6] In omni creato videmus trinum et unum Deum, quadam participatione; nam quanto creatura Deo similior, tanto magis trina et una. In omnibus infimis et supremis creaturis est essentia, virtus, et operatio. *Excit.*, viii (*Sanctus, sanctus, sanctus*), p. 601. Cf. *Excit.*, ii (*Fides autem Catholica haec est*), p. 385, and *Excit.*, v (*Paracletus autem Spiritus Sanctus*), p. 491. So precisely in Erigena and in Eckhart. Tria etenim sunt, quae in omni substantia, sive corporibus adhaerente, sive omni corpore absoluta, si tamen aliqua substantia est praeter Deum, quae sive intelligibili sive sensibili corpore careat, incommutabilia et inconversibilia permanent, essentia, virtus, et naturalis operatio. *De div. nat.*, v, 9 (881, A, vol. 122, ed. Migne). Wan ein ieglich werc vliuzet uz der kraft unde diu kraft vliuzet uz dem wesen. Pfeiffer, *Meister Eckhart*, p. 210. Aus allen wesen so fluzzet di craft in di werk. Jostes, *Meister Eckhart und seine Jünger*, p. 2.

uses a slight variation of it.[1]   Usually, however,
his terms are different, and he varies them considerably.[2]   His favourite triad is unity, equality,
and connexion.[3]   Unity is identified with Being
—this Eleatic principle is axiomatic in Nicholas's
system.   The terms are interchangeable.   The more
anything has unity, the more it has being,[4] and the
more it approaches ultimate unity and ultimate
being.   God is absolute Being and absolute Unity,
and as such is eternal and immutable.   But Unity
involves Equality, and involves Connexion.   God
is therefore, as *Ens entium*, eternally and immutably
One, but his Unity involves an eternal and immu-

[1] In Patre habent omnia essentiam, in Filio potentiam,
in Spiritu sancto operationem.   *De dato*, v, p. 289.
[2] Once the triad is *unitas, species, utilitas*.   *Excit.*, ii (*Fides
autem Catholica haec est*), p. 385.   This is manifestly a variation on Hilary's great phrase.
Eckhart has various triads of a more or less similar type.
Daz mugt ir merken an allen dingen, di da sint : di sint
niht von ir selber, mer si sint gesachet von einer sach, da
irs selbes ist, daz ist der vater : und aller ding bilde in im
hat, daz ist der sun ; minne ze dem selben bilden daz ist
der heiligeist.   Jostes, *Meister Eckhart und seine Jünger*, p.
16.   Wesen ist der vater, einikeit ist der sun, güete ist der
heilige geist.   Pfeiffer, *Meister Eckhart*, p. 124.
[3] Compare the language of Eckhart : Der sun ist glichnis
des vaters, ane daz, daz er enpfät von dem vater allez, daz
er hat, und alles werdennes ist er ein bilde.   Doch ist er
ein an dem entwerdenne.   Der heiligeist ist ein zesamenthalt
des vaters unde des suns.   Pfeiffer, *Meister Eckhart*, p. 497.
[4] Ens et unum convertuntur.   *De doct. ign.*, ii, 7, p. 31.
Omnia in tantum sunt, in quantum unum sunt.   *De ven.
sap.*, xxi, p. 314.   This thought is borrowed from Augustine,
De moribus Manichaeorum, vi (8).   Compare Eckhart's remark
(on the *Wisdom of Solomon*, 7, 27) in Pfeiffer, *Meister Eckhart*,
p. 613.

table Equality, and an eternal and immutable Connexion between His Unity and His Equality.

The whole universe is seen in the light of this conception of the Trinity. Things in this world are many, but they are ever seeking unity; they are different, but they are ever seeking equality; they are divided, but they are ever seeking connexion. Thus God, as Unity, Equality, and Connexion, is the final cause of all that exists. But this triune principle is the principle of the universe only in a reversed sense, and here is perhaps both the main difficulty and the main weakness of the Cusan system—for though unity involves multiplicity, and equality involves inequality, and connexion involves separation, these last are always thought of as a lapse from original perfection, and thus the world, which is in its very nature multiple and unequal and divided, is really a declension from the first principle. The very fact of existence as we know it is a degeneration from undifferentiated and undivided unity, and the whole history of things, once created, is the process of their instinctive and inevitable tendency to become one again, in that original unity in which there can be nothing of difference or division. That, taken by itself, is a possible and a consistent view of finite existence. But then, on the other hand, finite existence is represented by our philosopher as a necessary fulfilment of what is eternally implicit in the infinite, and the world is the most perfect reflection that is possible of the perfect nature of God. Now if the necessary development of what is eternally implicit in the nature of God is necessarily defective, if the most perfect manifestation of the nature of

God that is possible in the finite world is imperfect, it would appear that there is (to speak paradoxically) a defect in omnipotence, for it is limited by a defect that is inherent in the finite. There is a deep inconsistency between a view that represents the universe as the best possible expression of the perfect, and a view which represents the universe as a necessarily imperfect expression of the perfect, when the perfect is held in both cases to be the omnipotent. And both views are held in the philosophy of Nicholas.

A similar inconsistency runs through Nicholas's doctrine of evil. The most astonishing defect of his system, from both the theological and the metaphysical standpoint, is the extreme slightness of his treatment of this problem. Goodness and reality are equated, and it follows that what is evil is unreal.[1] It follows also that the evil can only exist in parasitic dependence upon the good.[2] The essential nature of every existing thing is good, as derived from God, and it is naturally only within the field of existence that evil can appear. It originates from an unnatural motion of the free will, in turning away from God.[3] The primary source of evil, in so far as it has a source, is the self-will of the Devil, who enviously desired to be as the Most High, and, through this impossible ambition, fell into a region of impossibility and

---

[1] Esse est bonum, et non esse malum. *Excit.*, vii (*Cum omni militia*), p. 557. Cf. *De ludo globi*, ii, p. 229.

[2] Omne malum in bono fundatur, sicut infirmitas in corpore, vitium in anima. *Excit.*, x (*Volo mundare*), p. 635.

[3] *Excit.*, v (*Suscepimus*), p. 504; *Excit.*, ix (*Ecce ascendimus*), p. 647.

unreality.[1]   The secondary or mundane source of
evil is the sin of Adam.   Why did God permit
Adam's sin, with all its dire consequences for
humanity ?   The answer lies in what our Lord
said about the man who was born blind—it was
that the glory of God might be manifested thereby.[2]   For God knew that He would bring good
out of the evil, and glory to Himself.   In one place
Nicholas discusses the question whether God
knows evil.   He says that some writers argue
(and he evidently has Erigena in mind) that as
God is the source of good He knows the good,
but as He is not the source of evil, He does not
know the evil.   At this point Nicholas expressly
dissents from Erigena's doctrine, for he says
definitely that God knows evil as well as good, as
the eye knows darkness as well as light, and that
if it were not so, the knowledge of God would
not be perfect.[3]   Erigena's position is that God
does not know evil, for if He did it would have a
real existence, since the knowledge of things in the

[1] *Excit.*, v (*Reliquit enim Diabolus, et ecce angeli*), p. 484.
[2] *Excit.*, vi (*Una oblatione*), p. 523.   Cf. *Excit.*, vi (*Qui
credit in Filium Dei*), p. 541.
[3] Dico Deum gloriosum cognoscere bona et mala (quia
alias perfecte non cognosceret) sicut oculus cognoscit lumen
et tenebras.   *Excit.*, ix (*Ecce ascendimus*), p. 646.   Here
Nicholas is following Eckhart.   Wie got daz boese erkenne,
daz in ime selber niht wesen hat, sunder ez ist ein beroubunge
des wesens ? . . .   Da von erkennet gotes verstentnüsse
alle sünde und übel in dem vorgenden bilde ir widerwertigen
tugende, niht in bilden der sünde, als die lügen erkennet
er in dem bilde der warheit. Pfeiffer, *Meister Eckhart*,
p. 327.   This is also the doctrine of St. Thomas : Malum
cognoscitur a Deo non per propriam rationem, sed per
rationem boni.   *Summa theol.*, I, q. 15, a. 3.

11

mind of God constitutes their real existence.[1]
Here Erigena is more rigorously logical than his
disciple, for Nicholas expressly teaches that evil is
mere privation of being, and expressly accepts
Augustine's doctrine that God does not know
things because they exist, but that they exist because
God knows them. That position is indeed fundamental to his whole system, and therefore the
representation of evil as within the knowledge of
God, however it may agree with the symbolism of
Scripture and with the working creed of practical
religion, is a profound philosophical inconsistency.
It is quite impossible to reconcile it either with
his own general principles or with his express
statements that evil is not from God and has no
entity.[2]

The general principle of the unreality of evil is,
of course, the doctrine of the Neoplatonists generally, and of Augustine, Erigena, and Eckhart in
particular. But the ease with which the doctrine
is assumed and the almost casual way in which
it is used by Nicholas is very striking. Rotta
writes of the *ottimismo cristallino* [3] of our philosopher, and not without reason. Nicholas never
seems to feel that the fact of evil is a grievous
enigma. His system might have been conceived
as the explanation of a world in which the prob-
lems of the infinite and the finite, the absolute and
the relative, the one and the many, were the only real
difficulties, and in which moral evil did not exist.

[1] *De div. nat.*, ii, 20 (559, B); ii, 28 (596, B, C, vol. 122,
ed. Migne).

[2] *Excit.*, ix (*Volo mundare*), p. 635.

[3] *Il Pensiero di Nicolò da Cusa*, p. 7.

It is a singular contrast in this respect to the system of Erigena, for the Scot wrestles with the problem of evil through long passages of his greatest work, and his answer, such as it is, abounds with paradox and inconsistency, of which he seems to be more or less uncomfortably conscious all the time. Nicholas never struggles with the difficulty at all; he seems perfectly satisfied to dismiss evil as a lapse from reality, exactly as a curve is a lapse from straightness and as multiplicity is a lapse from unity. This, of course, is also Erigena's essential doctrine,[1] but he evidently feels the immense difficulty of the problem, while Nicholas hardly seems to feel that it is a problem at all. The contrast is very marked.

While Nicholas thus teaches the unreality of evil, he makes it a fact that is almost necessarily involved in the very constitution of the universe, and ultimately, as it would seem, in the very nature of God. For the universe, being what it is, can only share the reality of being in varied and diminishing degrees. God does not give something separate from Himself; He gives His absolutely best gift, His absolutely greatest gift; He gives Himself, and He gives Himself universally. But that gift cannot be received as it is given. The

[1] In his doctrine of the non-reality of evil, he follows Erigena closely, even to the use of his exact phrases. Compare, for example, Nicholas's language in *Excit.*, x (*Volo mundare*), p. 635 : Infirmitas, peccatum, mors, et quaecumque talia mala non sunt a Deo; nihil enim habent entitatis. Quare a Deo, qui est ipsum esse, non sunt, with that of Erigena in *De Praedestinatione* (366, B, vol. 122, ed. Migne) : Peccatum, mors, miseria, a Deo non sunt. Eorum igitur causa Deus non est.

very reception implies a descent.[1] The infinite is received as the finite, the universal as the particular, the absolute as the limited. God is perfectly reflected in the Logos—*imago Dei invisibilis*—but in individual things the reflection of the Divine nature is more or less faithful according to the degree of their spirituality, or, what is precisely the same thing, the degree in which they possess unity, or, what is precisely the same thing again, the degree in which they possess real being. Thus the universe is a hierarchy of different degrees of reality. Both Erigena (who has practically the same thought) and Nicholas thus teach a doctrine of degrees of reality which approaches that of modern philosophers.

Now if it is possible, and indeed necessary, that in the scale of being things should be increasingly less and less like God, farther and farther removed from Him, it would seem to be almost inevitable that the descending scale should at some point pass out of the range of being and of goodness altogether, and lapse into unreality and evil. Evil is represented as unreal and uncreated, as arising within the sphere of humanity by a misuse of free will,[2] but it is almost impossible to resist

---

[1] Quoniam ipsa forma infinita non est nisi finite recepta, ut omnis creatura sit quasi infinitas finita, aut Deus creatus, ut sit eo modo, quo hoc melius esse non posset; ac si dixisset creator: Fiat, et quia Deus fieri non potuit, qui est ipsa aeternitas, hoc factum est quod fieri potuit, Deo similis. *De doct. ign.*, 2, ii, p. 25. This is directly from Eckhart. Dar umbe sprichet man: möhte der vater, er mahte sich selber. Want des niht enmac sin, so würket er sin gelich. Pfeiffer, *Meister Eckhart*, p. 150. See also *De dato*, ii, p. 286.

[2] Nam Deum mundum, atque hominem, ad sui imaginem,

the implicit suggestion that if finite existence falls away far enough from ultimate reality, it will fall away at last into nothingness ; that if goodness declines into smaller and smaller proportions it will finally decline into the mere negation of what is good.

Thus the scheme of Nicholas's thought seems to involve the existence of evil as almost, if not altogether, necessary, while at the same time it involves the view that the world is the best possible world, since the Eternal Goodness is essentially creative, and God seeks to impart Himself, as far as possible, to every created thing—as far as possible, that is to say, as far as the thing is capable of receiving God. The universe cannot be God, but it is as much like God as it is capable of being, and so with every individual thing in the universe : [1] each thing shares as much of the divine principle as, in the nature of the thing, it is possible for it to possess. In the *Apologia* Nicholas rather recedes from this position, and admits that serpents and the like are not good or beautiful in themselves, but he pleads that as parts of the universe they help to constitute the goodness and beauty of the whole.[2] It is obvious that there is a material difference between the two doctrines ; it is one thing to say that all things are good in themselves, in varying degrees, according to their capacity, and it is quite another thing to say that some things are not good

et ipsum bonum valde creasse, et peccatum per hominem in genus humanum, non per creantem intrasse. *De genesi,* p. 131.

[1] *De doct. ign.,* ii, 11, p. 25.

[2] *Apologia,* p. 68.

in themselves at all, but that they are made to contribute to an ultimate good. The question of moral evil is not brought into this particular issue. Nicholas does not argue, as he might have done, that the existence of noxious animals is only a part of the larger question of the existence of evil. He strives to meet the difficulty by simply shifting our gaze from the particular to the universal. In this he is following a line of argument which he found in Erigena,[1] and which Erigena derived from Augustine.[2] In another direction also the teaching of Nicholas seems logically to involve the ultimate necessity of evil. For he seeks to escape dualism by identifying opposites, all the way through. He does this on the highest scale of all. God and the world are not contraries, but correlatives, for the very thought of God and the very thought of the universe involve each other. What God is, as absolute, the world is, as concrete. What the world is as multiple and temporal and finite, God is as One and Eternal and Infinite. But an essential dualism is not really escaped. It is merely driven deep into the very source of all. The fact of the actual multiplicity and the actual finitude of the world is obviously not to be denied, and so the attempt to resolve it is made. But the attempt merely results in making the multiple implicit in the unity, the finite implicit in the infinity. The eternal unity involves alterity, the eternal equality involves inequality, the eternal connexion involves separation. Surely this merely means that instead of accepting a dualism as be-

[1] *De div. nat.*, v, 33 (953–4, vol. 122, ed. Migne).
[2] *Conf.*, vii, 13.

tween God and the universe, we posit a dualism
in the very nature of God. In His unity there is
both the possibility and the actuality (since the
possible and the actual are one in God) of all the
multiplicity and all the finiteness that the philosopher
is desperately seeking to escape. Instead of escap-
ing it he has made it necessary, ultimate, and
eternal, for he has implanted it in the essence of
the Deity. This ought logically to be the result
even with regard to evil. Evil is always regarded
as a lapse from goodness in exactly the same way
that multiplicity is a lapse from unity, and (though
this is never admitted or even faced by Nicholas)
it ought to follow that evil is implicit in the eternal
goodness as multiplicity is implicit in the eternal
unity.

There is also a good deal of inconsistency, as
well as much that is suggestive, in Nicholas's doctrine of possibility and actuality, and in his attempt
to relate these to the Persons of the Trinity. The
principle of possibility is identified with God the
Father, the principle of actuality with God the
Son, and the principle of union between these with
God the Spirit.[1] The actual presupposes the possible, the possible presupposes nothing. Thus the
actual is from the possible, as the Son is from the
Father; the possible, like the Father, is from nothing. All that may be in the Father, is in the Son,[2]

---

[1] Eckhart has a somewhat similar triad. Die heiligen
sprechent, daz in dem vater si mügentheit und in dem sune
glicheit und einunge in dem heiligen geiste. Pfeiffer,
Meister Eckhart, pp. 97–8.

[2] Duhem, *Études sur Léonard de Vinci* (Seconde Série),
pp. 110–11.

and through the Spirit is realized in the world of sense,[1] as the limited actualization of that absolute possibility and that absolute actuality through that absolute union. Everything in the world is therefore the result of these three factors, which are one. Actuality is equivalent to form, and possibility to matter, in the Aristotelian sense. The great error of Aristotle was that he regarded the third factor as privation, and not as union. In God, since all opposites coincide in Him, there is a perfect union of actuality and possibility. He is all that He can be, and His is therefore absolute actuality and absolute possibility in absolute union. But that precise and perfect coalescence of the possible and the actual is found nowhere but in God. Nothing contracted can be precise; it is always a more or less. It cannot attain the precision of the Absolute any more than material things can attain the precision of the geometer's ideal circles and ideal triangles. It is an imperfect representation of an ideal perfection. Therefore everything in the world is all that it can be practically, but not all that it can be ideally. In other words, it has only a limited actuality, because it has only a limited possibility, and there is only a limited union between these. The world is therefore the contraction (in Nicholas's dialect) of possibility and actuality, while God is the absoluteness of both. Hence, the world is all, as concrete, and God is all, as absolute.

This is probably one of the points at which the philosophy of Nicholas will strike a modern thinker as most suggestive, and it is here that it connects

[1] *De vis. Dei*, xix, p. 200.

with several tendencies in the most modern range of philosophical and theological thought. For the doctrine of the coincidence of contraries, in its highest application, means that actuality and possibility coincide in God; absolute actuality and absolute possibility are one and the same in the Absolute.[1] Possibility is one of the most slippery notions with which the mind can deal, but it would probably be true to say that modern philosophers are more and more inclined to agree that a naked possibility is nothing at all [2]—that mere possibility cannot exist. There must be some sort of actuality to contain the potentiality of anything else. Probably the conception of possibility always really means to the mind some sort of vague existence, which in other conditions would become another sort and a more definite sort of existence. That is to say, the conception of possibility is one way of representing mentally the inter-relatedness and interchangeability of things, the fact that nothing is static, isolated, and self-sufficient, but that there is universal change and universal connexion within the universe. In the more detailed aspect this is emphasized in Nicholas's doctrine of universal compenetration, *quodlibet in quolibet*. Now all this is curiously parallel to some of the philosophical results of the doctrines of modern physics, which, as a distinguished English philosopher has said, really mean the breakdown of the purely analytical method of treatment, so that ' no ultimate constituent is now intelligible except in its relation to the whole system

[1] Cf. Rothe, *Dogmatik*, pp. 77–8.
[2] *De doct. ign.*, ii, 8, p. 33.

within which it acts'.[1]   On the theological side
these conceptions in Nicholas mean a dynamic as
against an intellectualist conception of God : that
he thinks of God not as static and transcendent,
but as active and immanent, with a vital process
within the Divine life which is expressed in the
relation between the Persons of the Trinity, and
which is expressed again throughout the universe
as the possibility, the actuality, and the motion
which are unitedly present in every existing thing.

At this point, also, there is rather a singular
return to a typical position of Neoplatonism in the
Cardinal's later thought.   Toward the end of his
life the concept of the *posse fieri* takes on a new
importance and a new significance.   It becomes a
sort of intermediate stage of quasi-existence [2]
between God and the world of appearance, almost
like the κόσμος νοητός of the Neoplatonists, and
the *causae primordiales* of Erigena.   Nicholas illustrates the conception by the relations of light and
visibility and colour.   Light makes it possible to
see the hitherto unseen world—the world which
was possibly visible, but actually invisible—for
light makes colour, without which nothing can
be seen.   When it does this it makes the thing-
that-may-be-seen into the thing-that-is-seen, i.e.
the visible as the possible-realizable into the visible
as the possible-realized.   Now what colour is in
the material world, that the *posse fieri* is to the
whole universe.[3]   It is through it, as issuing from
God, that the possible becomes actual.   It is obvious

---

[1] Mackenzie, *Ultimate Values*, p. 28 (cf. p. 62).
[2] Hasse, *Nikolaus von Kues*, p. 67.
[3] *De ven. sap.*, vi, p. 302.

that nothing is made that could not be made; hence the world might have been made from all eternity, for the ground of its possibility was eternally in God. Therefore we must conceive a possible creation, or *posse fieri*. And if it were possible from all eternity for things to be made, there must have been that which could make them. Therefore we must conceive a possible Creator, or *posse facere*. Now there must be some bond, some connexion, between that-which-could-create and that-which-could-be-created, between the *posse facere* and the *posse fieri*, or else that which could create had never created, and that which could be created had never been created.[1] This bond is the universe, or *posse factum*, the existence of which constitutes the possible Creator the actual Creator, and the possible creation the actual creation.

It is true that Nicholas has previously taught that possibility and actuality coincide in God, but his thought here seems to be that there derives from God this emanation of the *posse fieri*, this half-created world,[2] so to speak, of the possible-actualizable, and that from this again is realized the world of appearance. For the possible only becomes the actual (in so far as both the possible and the actual are not solely in God) when it appears as the concrete, the phenomenal, and that only comes into appearance through the existence of this rather indeterminate and indescribable universe of the possible-realizable. The conception is difficult and

[1] *De mente*, xi, p. 165.
[2] Omnia in posse fieri confuse et complicite creata, quae postea facta et explicata leguntur. *De ven. sap.*, ix, p. 304.

attenuated enough, and it may well be doubted whether it adds anything of value to Nicholas's system.

Is this very difficult notion of *posse fieri* to be taken to represent, so to speak, the dynamic aspect of the Deity ? [1]   Or is it to be taken, with some of Nicholas's expositors, as equivalent to the πρώτη ὕλη of Aristotle or the formless matter of Augustine ? Thus it falls into line with the Trinitarian conceptions we find elsewhere in Nicholas's writings, where possibility or matter is identified with the Father, and actuality or form with the Son.[2]   Still it is difficult to understand the relation of the Spirit to this creative scheme, for the *posse factum* does not represent the uniting principle, but rather the thing actualized, the existent world ; or if it does represent the uniting principle it represents that principle actualized as the world, and nowhere else does Nicholas identify the Spirit with the universe in such a way.

One may well despair, in fact, of attaining either any consistent conception or any clear expression of this very elusive notion of *posse fieri*, or of its relation to the rest of the associated phrases. His description of it bristles with statements which contradict equally express statements found elsewhere in his philosophy. It is a kind of intelligible world between God and the material universe, and yet it is not, for there is no such intermediate

[1] Kaestner, *Der Begriff der Entwickelung bei Nikolaus von Kues*, in *Berner Studien zur Philosophie*, iv (1896), p. 21.

[2] But elsewhere Nicholas expressly says that before the *posse fieri* there is nothing but the *posse facere*.   *De ven. sap.*, xxxix, p. 330 ;   *De Possest*, p. 260.

existence.[1] It is a sort of formless matter, which is something, for it is subsequent to God, and prior to the world, though it is something that we cannot conceive any more than we can conceive the existence of God; and yet it is nothing at all, for matter without form simply has no existence.[2] In creating it God created all things in it, which afterwards develop into actual existence; yet no such world of creative form exists, for God is the one Form of all forms.[3] It is the germ of all the different germs of existence; yet the differences of actual existence are not due to any differences in germinal principles, but merely to an accident of existence.[4] In fact the whole conception is beset with hopeless inconsistencies, and only bewilders Nicholas's metaphysics; but it is interesting as a late development of his thought.

[1] *De mente*, xi, p. 165; *De ven. sap.*, xxxviii, p. 328; *De ludo globi*, i, p. 219; *De doct. ign.*, ii, 9, p. 36.
[2] *De ludo globi*, i, p. 219; *De dato*, xxii, p. 286.
[3] *De ven. sap.*, iii, p. 300; iv, p. 301; *De mente*, ii, p. 151; *De Possest*, p. 252.
[4] *De ven. sap.*, vi, p. 302; *De doct. ign.*, i, 17, p. 12; ii, 9, pp. 34-5.

CHAPTER IV

COSMOLOGY, AND THE INFINITE

THE cosmological doctrine of Nicholas is worked out by means of the notion of *contractio*, and the Trinitarian rhythm is found here, as everywhere else. Since the absolute unity is of necessity absolutely triune, so also the maximum concrete unity is necessarily triune, not absolutely, as the Trinity is Unity, but concretely, so that the unity only consists in the threefoldness —as the whole in the parts. Concreteness cannot exist without a contractable (*contrahibile*), a contracting (*contrahens*), and a connexion that fulfils itself in the common activity of both. This capability of concreteness (*contrahibilitas*) is possibility, which descends from the Divine Unity, and precedes all being. The contracting (*contrahens*) descends from equality of unity, as limiting the possibility. For equality of unity is equality of being, since unity and being are interchangeable terms. Last there is the connexion of the contracting and the contractable, or of matter and form, or of possibility and necessity, through the uniting Spirit of Love.

The possible only comes to actuality through actual being, since nothing can bring itself to actuality, for otherwise it would be the cause of itself, and be before itself.[1] Philosophers also agree, Nicholas says, that what brings possibility to actuality acts from purpose, so that possibility comes to actuality in a rational order and not by chance. This highest nature some call mind; some, the soul of the world; some, fate; some, like the Platonists, concrete necessity. These last believe possibility to be determined necessarily through itself, so that it now is in actuality what it could be before in nature.[2]

The philosophers say that all is in the world-soul, as the fruit is in the seed, and that it is developed and unfolded by motion. So the sculptor has the ideal form of the statue in his mind, but it is by the motion of his tools that he is able to give effect to his ideal in the stone. Thus the world-soul carries the forms of things in itself, and by means of motion brings them to actuality in matter. This motion is diffused through all, and is thus a spirit of connexion. It proceeds both from possibility and from the world-soul—from possibility, which is mere aptitude and desire, and from the world-soul, which has all forms within itself—and is a movement bringing the two together. Nature is therefore the aggregate (*complicatio*) of all things which exist through motion. How this motion is contracted from the universal to the particular may be illustrated by an example. When I utter a

---

[1] Sapientes omnes in hoc concordant, quod posse esse ad actu esse non potest nisi per actu esse deduci; quoniam nihil seipsum ad actu esse perducere potest, ne sit sui ipsius causa: esset enim antequam esset. *De doct. ign.*, ii, 9, p. 34. Cf. *Excit.*, vi (*Una oblatione*), p. 519.

[2] *De doct. ign.*, ii, 9, p. 34.

phrase, the words issue with a distinct movement, in a definite order—letters, syllables, words, the whole sentence—though the hearer does not separate the order in hearing it. So a graduated motion in all things descends from the universal to the particular, and is here contracted into a natural and temporal order. This motion or spirit (*motus sive spiritus*) descends from the Spirit of God Who through motion itself moves all things. It is this motion of loving connexion which leads all to unity, so that all things form one universe. But no movement can be the absolutely greatest, for that coincides with rest, that is to say, with God, Who comprehends all movement in Himself. In God there is one supreme level where motion is thought and where possibility, actuality, and connexion are one; and there is another level in corporeal things, of matter, form, and connexion, where motion is being.

God is the absolute maximum; the world or the universe is the concrete maximum. The concrete maximum, which has all that it is from the absolute maximum, is as much as can be like the latter. The concrete unity is unity contracted by plurality (*per pluralitatem contracta*), as, in other aspects of the universe, we may speak of infinity contracted by finitude, simplicity contracted by composition, eternity contracted by succession, necessity contracted by possibility, and so forth. God, in His immeasurableness, is neither in the sun nor in the moon, though He is what is absolute in them; similarly the universe is not in the sun nor in the moon, though it is what is concrete in them. And the absolute being of the sun is not other than the absolute being of the moon, which is God Himself, Who is the absolute being and essence (*entitas et quidditas*) of all things ; but the concrete essence (*quidditas contracta*) of the sun is other than that of the moon, because the absolute essence (*quidditas absoluta*) of a thing is not a thing itself, but the concrete essence is the thing itself. The concrete essence (*quidditas contracta*) of the universe is different in the sun and in the moon, hence the identity of the universe is in diversity, as unity in plurality. So, though the universe is not the sun, and not the moon, yet in the sun it is sun, and in the moon it is moon, but it is that without plurality or diversity. Universe means universality (*universum dicit universitatem*), that is, the unity of many. Humanity is not Socrates, nor Plato, but in Socrates it is Socrates, and in Plato it is Plato ; and so is the universe to all things. All entities which are parts of the universe, without which it could not be one, whole, and perfect, enter into being along with the universe—not first intelligence, then soul, then nature, as Avicenna and other philosophers teach. The architect thinks of the whole house, before he thinks of a wall as a part of it ; thus in the intention of God all enters into existence, first the universe, and then, in consequence, all that without which neither a universe at all, nor a perfect universe, could be. God is the absolute being of the universe ; the universe is that being contracted. So we may conceive how God, the supreme unity, is, by means of the universe, in all, and the plurality of things is, by means of the universe, in God.

This is the meaning of that word of Anaxagoras :

12

Everything is in everything (*quodlibet esse in quolibet*). God is in all, in the sense that all is in Him; He is in all by means of the universe; hence, all is in all, and everything is in everything. Every individual thing cannot actually be all, because it is limited; it limits all in itself, that all may be that individual thing. The All is not plural, because plurality does not precede the individual existence. The All without plurality precedes each thing in the order of nature. There is, therefore, no plurality in the *actual* individual thing, but the All is without plurality the thing itself. All in the stone is stone; in the soul, soul; in life, life; in reason, reason; in God, God. Every actually existing thing finds its rest in this, that all in it is itself, and itself in God is God.[1]

God as absolute Unity is the first unity; the universe is the second unity, which consists in plurality. The third unity is that of the genera; the fourth unity is that of the species. The first, absolute, unity comprehends (*complicat*) all absolutely; the first concrete unity comprehends all concretely (*contracte*); the second comprehends the third, which is the last, and so we come to the particular. Universals therefore exist in the order of nature in a graduated fashion, before the thing which is their actual concrete expression (*ante rem, quae actu ipsa contrahit, existunt*). And because the universe is concrete, and therefore only to be found explicit in genera, and genera only in species, and species only in individuals, the universe only attains actuality in individuals. So, according to

[1] *De doct. ign.*, ii, 5, pp. 28–30. Cf. Erigena, *De div. nat.*, ii, 2 (528, B, vol. 122, ed. Migne).

this conception, universals only exist in concrete actuality (*universalia non sunt nisi contracte actu*).[1]

Precise equality belongs to God alone ; hence all things else differ. There cannot be one motion equal to another, nor can one be the measure of another, for the measure and the measured necessarily differ. Hence, truth abstracted from the material, as reason, is equality, and cannot be found in things, which always have a defect. We can never reach the absolute maximum by ascending, or the absolute minimum by descending, for the ascent and descent are both endless ; things may be infinitely greater or infinitely less. Every part of the infinite is infinite ; it is really a contradiction to speak of more or less in relation to the infinite. In infinite number two is not less than a hundred. The absolute maximum is therefore the negative infinite, for it alone is what it can be to the fullest extent (*omni potentia*). The universe (which includes all that is not God) cannot be negatively infinite, but it is without limit (*sine termino*), and is therefore privatively infinite. In this sense it is neither finite nor infinite : it cannot actually be greater than it is, but this comes of defect. Though the universe might be greater in respect of the infinite power of God, which is unlimited, yet it cannot be greater in respect of itself, because this is restrained by the possibility of being, or matter, which is not actually extensible to the infinite. Hence the universe is unlimited (*interminatum*), for there is nothing actually greater to limit it. In this sense it is privatively infinite ;[2] there is nothing outside of it, to impose limits upon it.

[1] *De doct. ign.*, ii, 6, p. 30.   [2] Ibid., ii, 1, pp. 22–4.

The distinction between the two infinites was made by the Scholastics,[1] but Nicholas uses the conception of privative infinity in a different sense. With St. Thomas Aquinas the privatively infinite is the indeterminate, which nevertheless is always conceivably determinable, for it might be limited and ended by the imposition of form. With Nicholas it is the indeterminable, because nothing exists that can limit it: it possesses form, but on the largest possible scale, and nothing exists beyond it to restrict it, or to determine it further than it is already determined within itself and by itself. It must be confessed that this notion of a privative infinity is little, if anything, more than the notion of the undefined, the ἄπειρον of Greek philosophy. The place that it holds in Nicholas's thought is mainly that of a medium between the absolute infinitude of God, and the finitude of particular things.

The universe is triune, and it could not be a universe if it were not a unity of possibility, actuality, and uniting motion, none of which can exist absolutely without the other. Hence all things necessarily exist in diverse grades, so that in the whole universe no two things are perfectly alike, and nothing is so small as to reach the absolute minimum, or so large as to reach the absolute maximum. It follows that it is impossible for the world to have an immovable centre, for if it had, that would be the point where motion had reached

---

[1] It is the doctrine of St. Thomas Aquinas that the infinitude of God is negative, and not privative. See *Summa theol.*, I, q. 7, a. 1; I, q. 12, a. 1–2; I, q. 25, a. 2; I, q. 52, a. 2; I, q. 75, a. 5; I, q. 86, a. 2.

its absolute minimum and become rest, and since the maximum and the minimum coincide, the centre of the world would coincide with the circumference. But the world has no circumference ; if it had, it would have its beginning and end in itself, and the world would be limited in relation to something else, for outside the world would be another world of space, which is an impossible conclusion. Now since it is impossible that the world should have a corporeal centre and a definite circumference, the only centre and circumference of the world is God. And while it is not an infinite world, yet it cannot be conceived as a finite world, for it has no limits in which it is enclosed. The earth (*terra*), therefore, which has no centre, cannot be without movement, for that it must move is involved in the fact that it can be moved, less and less, to an infinite extent. It is plain, then, that the earth really moves, though we do not notice it, because we can only mark movement in relation to something which does not move. A man floating down a river in a boat would not be able to tell that he was moving, except that he can see the banks.[1]

In these conclusions Nicholas is a precursor of Copernicus [2] and Kepler,[3] and was not without

---

[1] Cf. Ludwig Lange, *Die geschichtliche Entwickelung des Bewegungsbegriffes*, in Wundt's *Philosophische Studien*, Bd. iii, pp. 350–1.

[2] J. R. Charbonnel, *La Pensée Italienne au XVIᵉ Siècle*, p. 470 ; Höffding, *History of Modern Philosophy*, i, p. 90.

[3] Kepler certainly knew Nicholas's writings : in the *Mysterium Cosmographicum* (one of his earliest works) he refers to the Cardinal as *divinus mihi Cusanus* (*Opera*, ed. Frisch, Frankfort, 1858, i, p. 122) and he cities him on astro-

of the earth, which extends to the circumference of fire, is very great. Though the earth is smaller than the sun, as we know from shadows and eclipses, yet we do not know how much the region of the sun is greater or lesser than the region of the earth : equal they cannot be, for no star can be precisely equal to another. Neither is the earth the least star, for it is larger than the moon, as eclipses show, larger even than Mercury, as some say, and perhaps than other stars. We are not to conclude that a star is of less worth because it is of less magnitude. We cannot know whether the region of the earth is of a more perfect or less perfect grade, in respect of the regions of the sun, the moon, and the other stars. The same applies to the earth as a dwelling-place. We cannot say that men, animals, and plants, which have their dwelling-place on the earth, are of a more ignoble grade than the dwellers in the sun and the other stars. For though it cannot be that so many heavenly spaces and stars are empty, yet the dwellers in another star cannot stand in any relation to the dwellers upon earth, and it is impossible that we should know them.

The corruption of things on the earth is no valid argument for its lesser worth, for the world is a universe, and every particular star influences every other ; and it is not proved that there is anything wholly corruptible, but rather that what is corrupted passes into another mode of being ; and there is no place for death,[1] since death seems to

---

[1] *Ut ait Virgilius*, says Nicholas. *De doct. ign.*, ii, 12, p. 41. I do not know any passage in Virgil which corresponds with this reference. Rotta also remarks (in his edition of

be nothing but the resolution of the composite into its component parts.

Such is the cosmology of Nicholas. One of the most significant points in it is that he departs from the whole Aristotelian conception of a qualitative difference between the region of the celestial and the region of the terrestrial. There is no quintessence, distinct from the four elements, to make the material structure of the stars different from that of the earth. The earth itself is a star, and the same laws of matter and of motion apply throughout the universe. It is here that Nicholas influenced Giordano Bruno so profoundly, and through the Nolan, the later cosmologies.

the *De docta ignorantia*, p. 114) : Non pare che questa frase sia in Virgilio. There is, of course, this very sentiment (and a similar line of argument) in Lucretius, *De rerum natura*, ii, 991–1011.

CHAPTER V

THE NATURE OF KNOWLEDGE

WHEN we pass from the cosmology of Nicholas to his doctrine of knowledge we find that it depends upon the same general principles as to the relation of the finite to the infinite. The infinite and the finite stand in no proportion to each other. By more and more it is never possible to reach the simple maximum, because a greater can always be found. Things exist in grades of likeness—in genera and species, in spatial and temporal relations, and so forth. No two or more things are so related and alike that they cannot endlessly be more alike. The finite understanding can therefore never know the truth of things precisely by means of likeness (*per similitudinem*). For truth is a neither more nor less; it is an indivisible entity [1] which nothing (that is not the truth itself) can measure precisely, as little as that which is not a circle can measure a circle, the very essence of which consists in a kind of indivisibility. Our understanding, then, cannot attain truth except in such a way that a more precise attainment of it is always possible; as by multiplying the sides of a polygon you endlessly approach a circle, but never reach it. We know

---

[1] Cf. *De beryllo*, xvi, p. 271.

nothing of the truth finally except that in its finality it is unattainable. The ' what ' (*quidditas*) of things, which is the truth of their being, remains a pure mystery.[1] Absolute truth is thus absolute necessity,[2] absolute actuality, the absolute maximum, and our understanding can approach it in endless degrees of nearness, but can never absolutely reach it. As the truth of things is the essence of things, it follows that we can never reach that essential reality by the way of reason.

It is obvious that the conclusion that there is no proportion between the infinite and the finite is inconsistent with one whole aspect of Nicholas's philosophy,[3] according to which the finite derives from the infinite, and the concrete unity derives from the absolute unity, and the unity of God is related to the unity of reason as that is related to the unity of the understanding, and so on, all these relations involving a more or less, since they involve degrees of reality, of value, and of truth. If those degrees are not in the nature of a proportion between the infinite and the finite, what is the meaning of language?

In this aspect the philosophy of Nicholas is a theory of knowledge,[4] and this is one of the angles from which his system is most interesting to the modern mind. The essential principle here is that all human knowledge is an approximation, and only an approximation, to the truth. The truth is absolute, and all knowledge is relative. There

---

[1] *De doct. ign.*, i, 3, p. 3.
[2] Lenz, *Die docta ignorantia des Nikolaus Cusanus*, p. 72.
[3] Falckenberg, *Grundzüge*, pp. 25 and 26.
[4] Ritter, *Die christliche Philosophie*, ii, p. 6.

can be no exact measure for truth, except truth itself, for truth is unique—it is a kind of ultimate indivisibility, and our knowledge is always a more or less. We cannot attain truth by our understanding, therefore, except in such an approximate fashion that a closer approximation is always possible. This principle, in its application to particulars, has a result that approaches the Kantian position, since the quiddity of any thing, which is both its essence and its truth, is always out of reach of the mind.

Nicholas's logical doctrine is intimately connected with his ontological doctrine. His philosophy is a theory of knowledge and a theory of existence, and both the one and the other are governed by the same conception, that is to say, by a postulate as to the relations of the infinite and the finite. The whole secret of existence is the presence of the infinite in the finite, of the absolute in the relative, of the universal in the particular, of the perfect in the imperfect. And the whole process of knowledge is a progress in an increasing proportion toward the infinite, the absolute, the universal, the perfect, which, as infinite, cannot have any proportion, and must remain unreached and unknown. As the created existence descends from the essential unity of God to variety, multiplicity, and contradiction, it descends also from the absolute truth of God to a mere image of the truth, a remote reflection of the truth.[1] Hence all our knowledge is *coniectura*,[2] an approximation to

[1] *De dato*, ii, p. 286.
[2] Consequens est omnem humanam veri positivam assertionem esse coniecturam. *De coniecturis*, i, 2, p. 76.

the truth, which is capable of closer approximation in infinite degrees, but which never reaches the absolute truth. All real wisdom is a profound apprehension of this, a learned ignorance, a wisdom which recognizes that it must strive endlessly toward a more perfect knowledge of the truth, and that such a knowledge is more and more possible, but that the absolutely adequate apprehension of final truth is impossible to finite minds in a finite world. It is this principle of the relativity and limitation of human knowledge, of course, which gives the point to the title of Nicholas's greatest work, and the variations upon the phrase which constantly recur in his writings, *docta ignorantia, sacra ignorantia,* and so on.[1]

It should be understood that Nicholas's theory of knowledge does not mean scepticism. He does not doubt or despair of the validity of knowledge. No philosopher, indeed, has ever had a more complete faith in reason. He believes that knowledge is entirely valid as far as it goes, but it is always limited and always relative. It approximates more and more nearly to the final truth, but finite knowledge is never really adequate to infinite truth. Our knowledge consists in the recognition

[1] There is a remarkable passage in Pascal which might serve as a summary of Nicholas's philosophy, at least as regards this main principle of it. ' Les sciences ont deux extrémités qui se touchent. La première est la pure ignorance naturelle où se trouvent tous les hommes en naissant. L'autre extrémité est celle où arrivent les grandes âmes, qui, ayant parcouru tout ce que les hommes peuvent savoir, trouvent qu'ils ne savent rien, et se rencontrent en cette même ignorance d'où ils étaient partis ; mais c'est *une ignorance savante* qui se connaît.' *Pensées,* p. 94.

of degrees of likeness and unlikeness ; it is a sorting out of things into more and more general kinds, which approximate more and more to the One, the Maximum, the Absolute. But the final truth is one, indivisible, ultimate, and knows nothing of multiplicity and difference and degree. As a criticism of knowledge, and an emphasis upon its necessary conditions and its necessary limitations, the system of Nicholas is a genuine prelude to much that is most characteristic in modern philosophy.[1]

The sense of *coniectura* in Nicholas's writings is obviously not that of our word conjecture. We mean by conjecture a guess at the truth, which may be true or may be false ; it does not carry with it any assurance of being even in the direction of the truth, though that is the intention of it. Nicholas means by *coniectura* a conclusion or a conviction which is perfectly true as far as it goes, but which does not go (and in the nature of things cannot go) far enough. It is true, but it is not adequate. The only possible suggestion of falsity about it lies in the fact that it might be more and more true, in infinite degrees. But it is not a venture at truth that may hit or miss ; it is a genuine approach to truth that does not fail in its aim, but only falls more or less short of the mark, as it must do, because that measureless mark is absolute, eternal, infinite truth. In short, all our knowledge is real knowledge, but it is all classed as *coniectura* in the dialect of Nicholas, because it is inadequate, and cannot be other than inadequate, while finite minds seek to understand infinite realities.

[1] Rossi, *Niccolò di Cusa e la Direzione Monistica della Filosofia nel Rinascimento*, p. 16.

The psychology of Nicholas centres in one or two principles which are extremely interesting and important. The objects of sense (*sensibilia*) are known first of all in a mere confusion. The senses recognize their existence, but do not discern their nature. That is the work of reason, and the senses are merely the instruments of reason. The senses can do no more than furnish the material upon which reason works.[1] Reason, in the process of discernment, gives birth to number, and it is from number that there derives a threefold principle, distinguishing, proportionalizing, and compounding. All things, as they are intellectually conceived, exist in distinction, in proportion, and in composition. Through these, reason creates a rational world. Sense gives only a confused manifoldness, which reason reduces to a unity by way of distinguishing between things, of comparing them together, and of blending them one with another. In all this the discursive reason acts upon the logical law of contradiction. But that law is only valid for reason. Exactly as reason (or what we should call the understanding) brings unity, by means of separating, contrasting, and merging things, into the confused medley perceived by the senses, so the intellect, which is the highest power of the mind, sees a higher unity in which all distinctions disappear,[2] the coincidence of contraries, the Absolute.

There is thus a hierarchy of faculties in the

[1] *De coniectura*, i, 10, p. 83.
[2] *Apologia*, p. 67. Cf. Erigena, *De div. nat.*, ii, 24; iv, 11 (578, D, 787, C, vol. 122, ed. Migne) on the relations of *intellectus, ratio, sensus*.

intelligence of man. Some of our senses need actual contact with the object of sense—such are touch and taste. Some are of a higher grade, and are able to reach the object of sense at a lesser or greater distance—such are smell, hearing, and sight. Then imagination represents objects that are not merely distant, but actually absent from the reach of all the senses. Then reason is a still higher faculty, and presents us with conclusions that (if left to themselves) sense could not reach and imagination could not represent. Then intellect, the highest power of all, is to reason what unity is to finite number: it sees all as one, for it sees all the difference and distinction of the sensible and rational world as merged into the absolute unity and identity of God.

Nicholas carries his characteristic doctrines of explication and compenetration into his psychology. Intellect descends into sense, and sense ascends into intellect. The use of any one faculty really implies the use of all. Where the intellect is defective, as in the case of the insane, the senses give deficient results, and the madman does not really see and hear aright. Where the senses are defective, as in the case of the blind and the deaf, the intellect gives deficient results, and persons born without sight and hearing do not possess the conceptions of colour and of sound. But where all the faculties are present, each penetrates the other, and the intellect in the reason is reason, in the imagination is imagination, in the senses is sense. For the unity of intellect descends into the alterity of reason, the unity of reason descends into the alterity of imagination, the unity of imagination descends into the alterity of sense. In the reverse direction, in the unity of the imagination the intellect unites the alterity of sensations, in the unity of reason the intellect unites the alterity of images, in the unity of intellect itself the intellect unites the alterity of reason. The intellect is the *complicatio* of reason, imagination, and sense, and these are the *explicatio* of intellect, in Nicholas's familiar terminology.

It may be remarked that Nicholas does not distinguish between imagination, *imaginatio* or *phantasia*, and memory, *memoria*.[1] He regards these as one faculty, the characteristic activity of which is to reproduce what is absent from the perception of the senses—absent either through distance of space or through lapse of time. Neither in the aspect of fantasy nor in that of remembrance can this faculty do anything but reproduce what has already appeared to the senses.[2]

In respect of the doctrine of innate ideas, Nicholas occupies a position which appears singularly modern. He tells us that Plato held that there are notions which are created with the mind, though the union of the body with the mind brings forgetfulness of them, until they are revived in the growth of knowledge, so that knowledge in the deeper sense is reminiscence ; but that on the other hand Aristotle taught that the mind is a *tabula rasa*. Nicholas holds that both these doctrines are wrong, and that the truth is that there is a power of abstraction and of judgement, *vis iudiciaria*,[3] which is born

[1] Memoria seu imaginatio. *De ludo globi*, ii, p. 234. Imaginatio seu phantasia. *Compend.*, iv, p. 241.
[2] *Compend.*, iv, p. 241. [3] *De mente*, iv, p. 153.

13

in the mind, but it is only with the help of the bodily senses that it can be exercised. This faculty can actually operate only upon a basis of sensible knowledge. Apart from the work of the senses it would remain merely a capacity of knowledge. But apart from that capacity the work of the senses would not bring knowledge at all. The whole of Nicholas's attitude, with its blend of the empirical and the transcendental, is a striking anticipation of Kant.

Nicholas carries the trinitarian rhythm into his theory of knowledge, as into everything else. There is a triune ground of all things, for all things subsist in multiplicity, magnitude, and composition, which derive from the eternal trinity of unity, equality, and connexion. And the human mind has a triune operation : it is the measure of number, of size, and of mixture, and it always seeks to reduce the multitude of things to a principle of unity, the greatness and littleness of things to a standard of equality, the manifold composition of things to a bond of connexion.[1] It is thus ever striving to resolve the universe into One, into the Oneness of God, which is triune, since it is Unity, and undifferentiated Unity, and undivided Unity. The mind of man is therefore an image of the mind of God,[2] for in the mind of God all things are implicit in Unity, and the human mind seeks to restore all things to unity by way of

[1] Est igitur mens nostra distinctiuum, proportionatiuum, atque compositiuum principium. *De coniecturis*, i, 3, p. 77.
[2] Sicut enim Deus est complicationum complicatio ; sic mens, quae est Dei imago, est imago complicationis complicationum. *De mente*, iv, p. 152.

thought. Thought is, in fact, a simplification, a unification; we generalize always more and more widely, we reduce individuals to species, species to genera, genera to universals, universals to the universe. The whole process of thought is a sorting out of the multitude of things into larger and larger classifications which all tend toward unity. Now unity is the measure of number, and the mind of God is the measure and the term of all things.[1] And so the human mind is a kind of measuring faculty; to know is to take the measure of things,[2] in relation to each other and to the whole; to establish the right proportion as between particular facts and as between each particular fact and the universe. A measure is necessarily more simplex than the thing measured, and so it necessarily reduces the complexity of things in bringing them to a common standard and thus again by so much reduces them to unity.

Human knowledge is a kind of creation, which does not really create anything absolutely new, but gives unity and intelligibility to all that is confusedly contained in the sense impressions.[3] The knowledge which comes by way of the senses is real knowledge, for it actually reaches and represents the sensible object,[4] and it is primary, for there is nothing in reason or in imagination that

[1] Mens igitur divina, mensura et terminus omnium, quia ratio et definitio sui et omnium. *De ven. sap.*, xxviii, p. 321.

[2] Cognoscere enim, mensurare est; mensura autem est simplicior quam mensurabilia : sicut unitas, mensura numeri. *De beryllo*, xxxviii, p. 284.

[3] *De doct. ign.*, ii, 6, p. 31. Cf. Erigena, *De div. nat.*, ii, 24 (581, A, B, C, vol. 122, ed. Migne).

[4] *Compend.*, x, p. 246.

does not come first of all by way of sense;[1] but it is formless until reason gives it form.[2] Thus the mind of man, in giving form to the confused medley of sense, may be said to exercise a creative faculty, for it reduces the chaos of sensible knowledge to the ordered world of reasoned knowledge. But this is only a secondary kind of creation; the infinite mind is formative in the absolute sense, the finite mind is merely conformative.[3] In the process of knowledge there are three stages,[4] with the Divine knowledge as the fourth and highest stage —we know things by means of the bodily senses in a mere confusion where truth is lost; we know things in the mind as they resemble the truth; we know things in the higher region of the spirit as they are true—not indeed the truth, but nevertheless true; and God knows all as the truth itself. This, again, is a unifying process, for the manifold

[1] Nihil in ratione, quod prius non fuerit in sensu. *De mente*, ii, p. 150. Nihil est in phantasia, quod prius non fuerit in sensu. *Compend.*, iv, p. 241.

[2] Sensus animae sentit sensibile, et non est sensibile, unitate sensus non existente, sed haec sentatio est confusa, atque grossa ad omni semota discretione. Sensus enim sentit et non discernit, omnis enim discretio a Ratione est, nam Ratio est unitas numeri sensibilis. *De coniecturis*, i, 10, p. 82.

[3] Videris dicere velle, mentem infinitam esse vim formativam absolutam, sic mentem finitam vim conformativam seu configurativam. *De mente*, iv, p. 152. Divina mens est vis entificativa; nostra mens est vis assimilativa. Ibid., vii, p. 158.

[4] Divine quidem, hoc est, prout res est veritas. Intellectualiter, hoc est, ut res non est veritas ipsa, sed vere. Animaliter, hoc est, ut res est verisimiliter. Corporaliter vero, etiam verisimilitudinem exit, et confusionem subintrat. *De coniecturis*, i, 6, p. 78.

of sense is resolved into the unity of ideas, the multiplicity of ideas is resolved into that spiritual knowledge of unity which is the very image of God in the soul, and this again is resolved into the absolute unity of God.[1]

All the way through, then, knowledge is the quest for unity. In this respect, knowledge has a parallel direction to being, for all being has a natural drift towards unity. All that exists has an instinctive desire to exist more perfectly, and perfection is unity.[2] The more perfect a thing is, the more real being it has, and the more real being it has, the more it is one, for being and unity are one and the same.[3] Thus, as any individual existence attains more unity, it fulfils its essential being more and more, and at the same time becomes less and less merely individual. So that the very apex of being is absolute unity, where the individual, as separate, ceases to be, and yet is more truly than ever, since the essential ground of every individual existence lies in the absolute unity. And so it is precisely in the process of knowledge. Knowledge is a movement from ' that ' to ' what ',[4] a sorting out of things into more and more general kinds. The very essence of knowledge consists in this comparison and classification of things, first in the direction of equality as between one thing and another, and thus at the same time in the direction of unity, since the more things are alike the

---

[1] Lenz, *Die docta ignorantia des Nikolaus Cusanus*, p. 40.

[2] *De doct. ign.*, i, 1, p. 1. Cf. Glossner, *Nikolaus von Cusa und Marius Nizolius als Vorläufer der neueren Philosophie*, p. 24.

[3] *De ven. sap.*, xxi, p. 314; *De doct. ign.*, ii, 7, p. 31.

[4] Falckenberg, *Grundzüge*, p. 49.

more they are one. But when knowledge reaches its climax it ceases to be, for without plurality and difference there can be no knowledge, so that the consummation of thought is the cessation of thought.

CHAPTER VI

THE THEOLOGICAL CONCLUSIONS

THE mystical doctrine of knowledge held by Nicholas has important consequences on the theological side of his system. It bears directly upon his eschatology, and also upon his doctrine of mystical union with God, or *filiatio*. In the first direction it results (largely under the influence of Erigena) in representing the ἀποκατάστασις, the return of all things into God, as by way of knowledge. Creation is a descent from the infinite to the finite, from unity to multiplicity, from absolute actuality to limited actuality. Knowledge is the reverse process :[1] it is an ascent from the finite, the multiple, with its limited actuality, to the infinite and the one, with its absolute actuality. Hence the being of things in our knowledge is a higher being than the mere existence of things in fact, and it is by way of knowledge, as an ascending process of simplification and unification, that things return into the primal unity of God.

Similarly, this conception of knowledge leads up to a doctrine of intuition, which is also a mystical union with God. It is by way of the knowledge of particular things that we reach a knowledge of the universe, and it is by way of a knowledge of the universe, as the concrete maximum and the con-

[1] Lenz, *Die docta ignorantia des Nikolaus Cusanus*, p. 26.

crete unity, that we attain an apprehension of God, as the absolute maximum and the absolute unity. The lowest stage of knowledge is the knowledge of sensible things, which is merely a confused mass of impressions. Reason gives form, distinction, and unity to this medley. Thence we rise to the apprehension of the unity of the universe, and this leads us to the unity of all things in God. God is therefore the summit of knowledge, but knowledge, in the usual sense, ceases at the height of infinitude, and becomes a mystical contemplation of God which is really a mystical union with Him. The soul attains the image of God,[1] which, as most directly derived from Him, returns to Him and becomes one with Him. This likeness to God, which is one with God, resembles the eternal generation of unity from unity, which is equality, and is actualized through it, and so it is a *filiatio*,[2] which resembles the filial relation between God the Father and God the Son. It may also be called a *deificatio*, θέωσις. Thus knowledge, in the highest reach of all, where it ceases to be knowledge as we know it, becomes a *visio intuitiva*, a *simplex intellectualitas*, a mystical contemplation of God which is union with Him, a *filiatio Dei*.

In the whole of this region the intellectualist character of Nicholas's philosophy, like that of Erigena, is very marked. Knowledge is ultimately

---

[1] Utitur autem hoc altissimo modo mens seipsa, ut est Dei imago, et ut Deus, qui est omnia, in ea relucet, scilicet quando, ut viva imago Dei; ad exemplar suum se omni conatu assimilando convertit. *De mente*, vii, p. 159.

[2] Nihil igitur aliud est omnia cognoscere, quam se similitudinem Dei videre, quae est filiatio. *De fil. Dei*, p. 126.

one with unity and with reality. The return of all things to God is by way of knowledge; to love God is to know God; knowledge is the explication of faith,[1] the essence of eternal bliss consists in the knowledge of God. In this Nicholas is in line with one definite school of medieval thought. It was a question with the Scholastics whether the beatitude of the redeemed soul consisted in knowing or in loving God. St. Thomas Aquinas decided for knowledge, like Nicholas. Duns Scotus took the opposite side.[2] There can be no doubt that in the religious sense the great defect of the system of Nicholas (like that of Erigena) is that it emphasizes knowledge and neglects love as the spiritual principle of all religion, with the result that the Cusan philosophy as a whole takes on a character of Gnosticism.

The eschatology of Nicholas, as has already been said, is worked out in part by way of his conception of knowledge, as representing the reduction of all to the primal unity. But it is also partly worked out, on the more objective side, by his doctrine of Christ. The whole Christology of Nicholas depends upon two conceptions, of the universe as the concrete maximum, and of humanity as the middle term of creation. The Logos is

[1] Occasionally Nicholas gives the higher place to faith, as in *Excit.*, ii (*Fides autem Catholica haec est*), p. 385. Altior fides est quam intelligere.

[2] *Summa theol.*, i, ii, q. 3, a. 5. *Reportata*, qu. iv, n. 5. See Gilson, *Le Thomisme*, pp. 224–5, and Bertoni, *Jean Duns Scot*, p. 399. Compare the language of Eckhart: Minne mac niht anders haften denne in bekantnisse. Pfeiffer, *Meister Eckhart*, p. 84. Dar umbe ist daz bekantnisse bezzer, wan er leitet die minne. Ibid., p. 121.

represented as the creative principle, but the larger emphasis is upon Christ as the God-man, the climax of humanity, and therefore as the uniting point and principle of the universe.[1]

The unity of the universe is unity in multiplicity; hence everything in it is distinguished into opposing grades, and nothing coincides with anything else. No concrete grade can possibly participate precisely in any other; it exceeds it or is exceeded by it. Nothing concrete, therefore, since it can be more or less concrete, can ever reach the limit (*terminus*) either in the universe, in genera, or in species. The first general contraction of the universe is into the plurality of genera, and genera exist as concrete only in species, and species only in individuals, which alone exist in actuality. And no individual exists that is not beneath the summit (*infra terminum*) of its species, so that no individual can reach the highest in its species, or in its genus, or in the universe. No individual is so perfect in its species that it could not be more perfect, and none so imperfect that it could not be more imperfect; none therefore reaches either the highest or the lowest limit of its species. There

[1] This betrays very markedly the influence of both Erigena and Eckhart. Universalis quippe totius creaturae finis Dei Verbum est. *De div. nat.*, v, 20 (893, A, vol. 122, ed. Migne). Tota itaque humanitas in ipso, qui eam totam assumpsit, in pristinum reversura est statum, in Verbo Dei videlicet incarnato. Ibid., v, 36 (978, D). Cf. v, 39 (1019, A–1021, B). Kristus sprichet ' ist, daz ich erhaben wirde, so wil ich alliu dinc an mich ziehen '. Da meinet er : ob er über unser herze unde verstentnisse erhaben werde, so wil er uns nach im ziehen. Nach disem sint alle creature ein mensche unde der mensche ist got. Pfeiffer, *Meister Eckhart*, p. 522.

is really only one limit of all, whether of species, of genera, or of the universe; and it is the centre, circumference, and connexion of all; the universe does not exhaust the infinite greatness of the power of God, so as to form, as a mere maximum, the limit of that power. The universe does not reach the term of the absolute maximum, nor genera the term of the universe; nor species the term of genera; nor individuals the term of species; and all things are what they are in the best mode between the greatest and the least; and God is the beginning, the middle, and the end of the universe, and of every individual, so that all things, whether ascending or descending, or tending to the middle, approach God.

Among the genera, which are the concrete expressions of the one universe, there is such a connexion of lower and higher that where they meet they coincide. The highest species of one genus coincides with the lowest species of the next higher genus, and so there is one continuous perfect universe. So numberless species progress from the minimum, or from the maximum with which it coincides, so that there is nothing in the universe which does not possess a certain singularity that is found in none other.[1]

This is the point of departure of the peculiar Christology of Nicholas, which represents Christ as the maximum of humanity. Generally, the maximum of any species does not exist, because before the maximum is reached the species passes into another, and so the universe is continuous and the only concrete maximum that exists is the

---

[1] *De doct. ign.*, iii, 1, pp. 43–5.

universe. But if, as a unique exception, humanity should attain its concrete maximum in an individual, that individual would be one with the concrete maximum of the universe, and therefore one with the absolute maximum, as the concrete form of it. Humanity does actually reach this maximum in Christ, and therefore the universe exists in Him, and He is one with God. The details of the doctrine are worked out in the following way. If we think of the concrete maximum in any species as actually existing, it would be, according to the character of the given species, actually all that is contained or can be contained in that species. It would be the highest possible perfection, according to the given concreteness : hence there could be no greater, and as the greatest and the least coincide, it must encompass infinitely the whole nature of the given concrete. But it is manifest that this concrete maximum cannot possibly subsist as pure concrete, for nothing concrete can reach the highest perfection within the range of its genus or species ; and nothing concrete, as concrete, can be God, Who is absolute. The concrete maximum must necessarily be God and the creature, absolute and concrete, in one contraction. Now if the absolute maximum so unites the concrete with itself that it could not be more united, and thence what is so united, retaining the nature of the concrete, is the concrete and created perfection of a particular species, this wonderful union will surpass the reach of our reason, and such is the union of God and man in Christ. It is not a union of opposites, nor a union of what was before separate, nor a union of parts into a whole, for the nature of

God has no opposite, and knows no before and after, and has no parts. It is God as Creator and creature, without confusion and without composition.

There are innumerable grades of being in the universe. Some natures are inferior, like those which lack life and intelligence; some are superior, like the angels; and some are in the midst, between the one and the other. Now the absolute maximum is the being of all things, in the most universal fashion, and not more the being of one thing than of another; it is clear, then, that that being is most akin to the maximum which is most closely related to the universality of being. Hence it is the middle nature, which is the medium of connexion between the lower and the higher, and that alone, which is most fit to be raised to the maximum through the power of God. As the highest of the lower natures, and the lowest of the higher natures, it encompasses all natures in itself, and when it is brought into union with the greatest, the whole universe, in every possible mode and in the highest grade of perfection, subsists in it. Human nature is thus raised above all the works of God; it is the union of the intellectual and sensible natures, constricting the universe in itself, whence the ancients rightly named it *microcosmus*.[1] Lifted into union with the greatest, it is the fullness of the perfection of the whole universe and of all individual existences in it, so that in humanity all reaches its

[1] *De doct. ign.*, iii, 3, p. 46. See also *De ludo globi*, i, p. 217, and *Excit.*, v (*Suscepimus*), p. 505. Cf. Erigena, *De div. nat.*, ii, 5; iv, 8; v, 20 (531, B, 773, D, 893, C, vol. 122, ed. Migne).

highest level. But humanity does not exist except as concrete in this or that man. It is therefore necessary that one actual man should ascend to union with the greatest, so that he should be both God and man, the perfection of the universe, holding the primacy in all things. Through this One all things receive the beginning and the end of existence; through Him all passes over into the finite, and through Him all returns into the infinite. God, as the equality of all being, is the Creator of the universe. The absolute equality of being is united with the nature of humanity, so that God, through the assumption of humanity, is, in the sphere of humanity, all that is concrete, as, absolutely, He is the equality of all being. That man, therefore, who subsists through union with the greatest equality of being, is the Son of God, the Eternal Word, through Whom all is made, or the equality of being itself. We do not find in any creature a limit, so that it would not be possible for infinite power, in respect of any such given creature, to create a better and more perfect creature. But if a man is elevated to union with that power itself, so that he is no longer a creature subsisting in himself, but in union with infinite power, then that power is not limited by the creature, but only by itself.[1]

Such is the Lord Jesus Christ, the Son of God, the firstborn of all creation. In Him is the unity and the totality of all the virtues that are found separately and partially in the saints. He forgave sins, raised the dead, ruled the spirits, the sea, and the winds, and gave a law that is the perfect fulfil-

[1] *De doct. ign.*, iii, 3, pp. 46-7.

ment of every law. These, and many other things, witness that He is God and man.

God and man and every creature that could be created (*omnia creabilia*) exist in the highest and most perfect manhood, so that the whole fullness of God dwells in Jesus. This may be illustrated by the example of knowledge. Sensible knowledge is concrete; intellectual knowledge is universal. Man, as man, is intellect, where the sensible nature is supported by the intellectual nature, since the intellectual nature is a divine, separate, abstract being, while the sensible nature remains temporal and corruptible, according to its character. Thus we must think of our Lord. His humanity is supported by His Divinity, for otherwise it could not exist as the maximum of humanity. The intellect of our Lord, in its absolute perfection and its absolute actuality, must be personally supported by the Divine Reason, which is all that exists in infinite actuality.

The Eternal Word, the Son of God, Who is the fullness of all, since He could not be known to us otherwise than in a sensible form similar to ours, manifesting Himself according to our capacity, is clothed with human nature by the Holy Spirit.

Now man is begotten of the seed of Adam in fleshly lust, so that through propagation the animal conquers the spiritual; thus human nature because of its origin remains utterly incapable of transcending the temporal for the spiritual. But in Christ the human nature is not of the will of the flesh: it is born of God, and therefore there is no obstacle to hinder it from returning to the Father. Therefore in Christ human nature is exalted by union with God, and delivered from the weight of earthly desires. Christ took upon Him all the sins of human nature that draw us down to earth, that He might purge them and slay them. The Death of Christ on the Cross was representatively the extinction of all the carnal desires of human nature, and the satisfaction for all the sins of men.

The human nature of Christ is the maximum of human nature, and encompasses the whole range of the genus, and is in respect to every man the equality of being, so that Christ is much more fully united with every man than his friend or his brother. In every man who clings to Him with a living faith, Christ *is* that man, in the most perfect union. Hence the faithful are circumcised in Him, baptized in Him, dead in Him, raised in Him, glorified in Him, and united with God in Him. Christ could only bring mortal man to the glory of the Father, which is immortality because it is absolute life, by the mortal putting on immortality. This was only possible through death; for how could the mortal put on immortality, except it were stripped of mortality? and how could this happen, except the tribute to death were paid? So Christ died, and with Him human nature rose again to perpetual life, and the animal and mortal body became a spiritual and incorruptible body.

The humanity of Jesus, as the concrete appearance of the man Christ, must be thought of as united with the Godhead, and, as so united, it is absolute; so far as Christ is thought of as truly man, it is concrete, as through humanity He is man.[1]

[1] *De doct. ign.*, iii, 7, p. 53.

So the humanity of Jesus is the medium between the pure absolute and the pure concrete. He is a human God, and a Divine man.[1] Christ is the first-born from the dead, for before Him no man could rise again, since human nature had not yet reached in time to the maximum, united (as in Christ) with incorruptibility and immortality. At the Last Day the good and the evil alike will rise again, for Christ has brought human nature to incorruptibility. But it is not all men who will be glorified through Christ, the Son of God; it is only those who are Christ's, by faith, hope, and love. There is no perfect religion, leading men to final peace, which does not hold Christ as the Mediator and the Saviour; God and man; the Way, the Truth, and the Life. He is the perfection of human nature, and human nature is an essential part of the universe, without which the universe would not only not be perfect, but would not be a universe at all.

It has been remarked by Dorner,[2] with real insight, that the great defect of Nicholas's Christological doctrine lies in the fact that he had not arrived at 'a knowledge of the significance of human personality, and to that knowledge none can attain who take as little notice of sin as did Nicholas of Cusa'. Every one who possesses any religious instinct must feel that Nicholas's doctrine moves throughout in a region of bloodless abstractions, and the reason undoubtedly is that he took so light a view of the fact of evil. It is impossible for a

[1] Verbum enim Dei es humanatum et homo es deificatus. *De vis. Dei*, xxiii, p. 204.
[2] Dorner, *Doctrine of the Person of Christ*, ii, pp. 46-7.

man who feels the profound poignancy of the problem of evil in the world, or, we may add, who feels sin to be a grievous burden and blight in his own life, to dissolve the great facts of redemption into a series of philosophical categories.

From this point Nicholas passes on to eschatological and sacramental doctrine. As God and man, Christ is the Judge of humanity. He is the supreme reason, and all reason derives from Him. It is the very character of reason to make distinguishing judgements. So rightly Christ is the Judge of the living and the dead. It is manifest that no mortal can comprehend that final judgement and that final sentence, for it is beyond all temporal and mundane conditions. God is the infinite light, and in Him the present and the past, the living and the dead, are all comprehended (*complicat*), as physical light is the hypostasis of all colours. Christ is as the purest fire, which is inseparable from the light and subsists not in itself but in the light; and, as this fire, He proves and judges all. All rational spirits are judged in Christ, as combustible things are tested in the fire (*quasi ignibile in igne*). Some things in the fire are changed into the very likeness of the fire, as the best gold in the heat of the fire seems to be no longer gold but fire itself.[1] Other things, such as silver, brass, and iron, do not participate so much in the intensity of the fire. Yet all appear as changed into fire, but each in its own grade of likeness. So all spirits

[1] He uses this metaphor again in *Excit.*, ix (*Ite et vos in vineam meam*), p. 644. It was a favourite with Erigena also, and is borrowed from him. The first source appears to be Origen, *De princ.*, ii, 6.

are judged in Christ, and so God is all in all, and all is in God, as far as that is possible, according to the capacity of each.

Now the light of God is itself eternity and truth, and so the rational creature, which desires to be illuminated by it, must be converted to the eternal and the true, above the mundane and the false. Corporeal and spiritual things are of a contrary mode. The corporeal is vegetative, and changes the nourishment received from outside into the nature of the nourished; it does not change the animal into bread, but the converse.[1] The intellectual spirit, whose activity is above time, as on the horizon of eternity, cannot change the eternal into itself, for the eternal is immutable, neither can the spirit, since it is incorruptible, be so changed into the eternal that it ceases to be an intellectual substance. But it is so changed that it is absorbed into the similitude of the eternal, yet with degrees of difference.[2] The intellectual nature, beyond time and beyond corruption, moves by a natural motion towards the most abstract truth, as to its last desire and its last object, which is God; and the immortal and incorruptible intellect is unsatisfied until it reaches Him. As it is eternal life at last to know the eternal God, which is the constant

[1] This is evidently suggested by a passage in Eckhart. Wan diu lipliche spise, die wir in uns nemen, diu wirt gewandelt in uns; aber diu geistliche spise, die wir enpfahen, diu wandelt uns in sich. Pfeiffer, *Meister Eckhart*, p. 31.

[2] *De doct. ign.*, iii, 9, pp. 55-6. In the whole of these eschatological passages, Nicholas is closely dependent upon Erigena, especially *De div. nat.*, v, 36-40 (960-1022, vol. 122, ed. Migne).

desire of our nature at its best,[1] so it is eternal death to be eternally separated from the fulfilment of that desire, and to be cast down into that chaos of confusion where eternal fire torments. God does not will the death and damnation of the sinner, which is the penalty of sin, *as* death, or *as* damnation, or *as* penalty : He wills it as justice (*non sub ratione peccati vel damnationis, sed sub ratione iusti*).[2] But both eternal life and eternal death are beyond our comprehension except by way of signs and symbols.[3]

Faith is the beginning of wisdom. In every faculty there is some thing presupposed as a first principle, which can only be apprehended by faith. Faith comprises in itself all that may be known : knowledge is the explication of faith.[4] There is no more perfect faith than the truth itself —the truth as it is in Jesus. He is the end of all knowledge, as truth ; of all sense, as life ; of all being (*esse*), as entity (*entitas*) ; He is the perfection of every creature, as the God-man. And faith unites the believer with Christ and makes us one with Him.

With regard to the sacraments of Baptism and the Eucharist Nicholas is more liberal than might be expected in that generation. Baptism is the sacrament of faith. But the spiritual fact is of greater importance than the mere sign. For where a man has faith and cannot have Baptism

---

[1] Maximum unum per se bonum ab omnibus desideratur. *De ven. sap.*, viii, p. 303.

[2] *Excit.*, vii (*Haec est voluntas Dei, sanctificatio vestra*), p. 575.

[3] *De doct. ign.*, iii, 10, pp. 56–7.

[4] Ibid., iii, 11, p. 57. The printed texts read *complicatio*, which is manifestly wrong.

(as the dying robber on Calvary) faith is enough.[1]
The Eucharist is the sacrament of the Word.
Under the appearance of corporeal food the believ-
ing soul receives that spiritual food of the soul
which is the Word of God. And the sacrament
of the Word depends in a way upon the preaching
of the Word, for how can the elements in the
Eucharist be the living Bread to a man's soul unless
he has been taught by the living Word?[2] Here
too faith is the necessary factor. For the Eucharist
is a sacrament in which we receive the Bread of
Life by faith. Apart from faith that it is such,
we do not receive it as such. Received by little
children who are unable to distinguish between
the corporeal and the spiritual food, or by Jews and
unbelievers who are without faith, it would not
be truly received.[3] The spiritual reception of
Christ in the Eucharist depends entirely upon the
faith of the recipient.

It will be seen that Nicholas's doctrine of faith
is rather strikingly evangelical for his age. He
teaches expressly that faith is the presence of the
power of Christ Himself in the soul of the believer.[4]
The Word of God dwells in our souls through
faith—that Word through which the heavens were
created. Therefore faith surpasses all natural
possibility, and to the believer all things are possible. Faith begets hope, and love arises out of
faith and hope.[5] Yet love is the life of faith,

---

[1] *Excit.*, x (*Assumptus est in coelum*), p. 672.
[2] Ibid., ix (*Loquere et exhortare*), p. 626.
[3] Ibid., v (*Promisi hodie*), p. 489.
[4] Ibid., viii (*Puella surge et resurrexit*), p. 612.
[5] Ibid., v (*Quotquot tangebant eum, salvi erant*), p. 506.

and the form (*forma*) of faith,[1] and gives it being, for love is the living principle of all the virtues.[2] Thus we are united with Christ in this life by faith and love, and the unity of those who believe in Christ and love Him is the Church. This ecclesiastical unity is resolved by Christ into that absolute unity of God from which it began, through the absolute Union (*unio*) which is the Holy Spirit.[3]

With this last phrase our study of the system of Nicholas of Cusa may very well end. For it is entirely characteristic of him. The whole of his thought, political, philosophical, and theological alike, is marked by a persistent method of intellectual reconciliation and by a passion for unity. He was the advocate of unity in the political system of Europe; he was the apostle of unity amid the ecclesiastical dissensions of Christendom; and he was the philosopher of unity also, who consistently sought to see the beginning and the end of all things, the real essence and the real significance of all existence, as hidden in the superessential Unity of God.

[1] Amor, qui est forma, dans complementum fidei. *Excit.*, iv (*Confide filia, fides*), p. 461.

[2] *Excit.*, iv (*Confide filia, fides*), p. 464.

[3] *De doct. ign.*, iii, 12, p. 62.

INDEX

Actuality, 114
Aeneas Sylvius, 28, 33, 65
Ainsdorfer, Caspar, 92
Alcinous, 93
Alphonso X of Castile, 86
Amalric of Bena, 90
Ambrose, St., 19, 81
Anaxagoras, 139, 167
Annenberg, Percival von, 62
Anselm, St., 81, 120, 125, 127
Aquinas, St. Thomas, 51, 81,
      109, 112, 136, 141,
      151, 170, 191
Aristotle, 7, 81
Athanasius, St., 19, 81
Augustine, St., 19, 81, 91,
      109, 110, 112, 126,
      144, 146, 148, 152,
      156
Averroism, 7
Avicenna, 167
Avignon, 9

Bacon, Roger, 25
Balbus, Peter, 93
Basel, Council of, 8, 12, 14–
      27, 32, 34, 36, 50, 66,
      89
Being, theory of, 102–8
Beldomandi, Prosdocimo de',
     5
Benzi, Ugo, 5

Bessarion, 2, 31, 32, 36, 75
Boethius, 81
Bracciolini, Poggio, 36
Bregno, Andrea, 79
Briçonnet, Denys de, 85
Brockhaus, C. F., 66
Bruno, Giordano, 175
Bursa Cusana, 82
Bussi, Giovanni Andrea, 78,
     93

Calendar, reform of the, 24–6
Cantor, 5, 119
Carvajal, 40, 75
Cesarini, Julian, 5, 14, 19, 20,
     22, 23, 30, 88
Charbonnel, J. R., 134, 171
Charles V of France, 12
Charles VI of France, 10
Christology, 193–200
Chrysostom, St. John, 81
Coincidence of contraries,
     122–43
collagium, 47
Cologne, University of, 7
Columbus, 94–5
Compactata, the, 24, 75–6
complicatio, 132, 183
Concubinage, 46–7
coniectura, 114, 178–80
Conrad of Wartburg, 89
Constance, Council of, 11, 12

205

Printed in Great Britain by
Butler & Tanner Ltd.,
Frome and London

GREAT MEDIEVAL CHURCHMEN

JOACHIM OF FLORA

By

HENRY BETT, M.A.

6s. net

"Mr. Bett's treatment of his subject is singularly able : it ranks with the best short monographs of our time. Clearly written, well arranged, accurate, it carries the reader along irresistibly."—*Saturday Review*.

"Mr. Bett has produced a learned book."—*Methodist Recorder*.

"Mr. Bett has provided an illuminating volume on the Italian mystic."—*Catholic Historical Review*.

INNOCENT III

By

L. ELLIOTT BINNS

D.D., F.R.Hist.S.

6s. net.

"A lively and well-balanced little book."—*The Times Literary Supplement*.

"He picks his way through the complications with an agility and an economy of words which makes one gasp with admiration. . . . If the other volumes in this series are as good as this, it should be a memorable series."—*Observer*.

"An admirable portrait."—*Church of England Newspaper*.

"This volume is a worthy attempt to give readers an insight into the tangled history of the thirteenth century."—*Listener*.

METHUEN & CO. LTD. LONDON